Algrove Publishing Limited
36 Mill Street, P.O. Box 1238
Almonte, Ontario, Canada K0A 1A0

Telephone: (613) 256-0350
Fax: (613) 256-0360
Email: sales@algrove.com

National Library of Canada Cataloguing in Publication

Beard, Daniel Carter, 1850-1941.
    Boat-building and boating / by D.C. Beard.

(Classic reprint series)
    Reprint. Originally published: New York : C. Scribner's Sons, 1911.
    ISBN 1-894572-75-0

    1. Boatbuilding. 2. Boats and boating. I. Title. II. Series: Classic reprint series (Almonte, Ont.)

VM321.B38 2003   623.8'2   C2003-901448-7

Printed in Canada
#1-2-04

Publisher's Note

In 1911, when Dan Beard finished writing this book, the world was still adapting to electricity and internal combustion engines. It was common to use people power alone to make things and the same source of power to move those things around. The text reflects that reality as well as reflecting Dan Beard's boundless optimism. He encouraged Boy Scouts to create a different reality for themselves by encouraging them to make things that would bring interest and excitement to their lives.

Not all his suggestions were wise. As one example, the Chump's Raft on page 15 might have seemed like a good idea at the time, but it is neither a method nor an apparatus likely to be used today. Discretion is advised in following Dan Beard's suggestions; time, technology and the collective experience of the intervening century often indicate other paths.

Leonard G. Lee
Publisher
February 2004
Almonte, Ontario

Bound for a good time

Boat-Building and Boating

By

D. C. BEARD

With Many Illustrations
by the Author

NEW YORK
1911

Algrove Publishing
Classic Reprint Series

AFFECTIONATELY
DEDICATED TO THE MEMORY OF
TOM AND HI

PREFACE

THIS is not a book for yacht-builders, but it is intended for beginners in the art of boat-building, for boys and men who wish to make something with which they may navigate the waters of ponds, lakes, or streams. It begins with the most primitive crafts composed of slabs or logs and works up to scows, house-boats, skiffs, canoes and simple forms of sailing craft, a motor-boat, and there it stops. There are so many books and magazines devoted to the higher arts of ship-building for the graduates to use, besides the many manufacturing houses which furnish all the parts of a sail-boat, yacht, or motor-boat for the ambitious boat-builder to put together himself, that it is unnecessary for the author to invade that territory.

Many of the designs in this book have appeared in magazines to which the author contributed, or in his own books on general subjects, and all these have been successfully built by hundreds of boys and men.

Many of them are the author's own inventions, and the others are his own adaptations of well-known and long-tried models. In writing and collecting this material for boat-builders from his other works and placing them in one volume, the author feels that he is fulfilling the wishes of many of his old readers and offering a useful book to a large audience of new recruits to the army of those who believe in the good old American doctrine of: " If you want a thing done, do it yourself." And by doing it yourself you not only add to your skill and resourcefulness, but, what is even more important, you develop your own self-reliance and manhood.

No one man can think of everything connected with any one subject, and the author gratefully acknowledges his indebtedness to several sportsmen friends, especially to his camp-mate, Mr. F. K. Vreeland, and his young friend, Mr. Samuel Jackson, for suggestions of great value to both writer and reader.

DAN BEARD.

FLUSHING, L. I., *Sept.*, 1911.

CONTENTS

Fig. 1.—The logomaran.

BOAT-BUILDING AND BOATING

CHAPTER I

HOW TO CROSS A STREAM ON A LOG

How to Build a Logomaran

THERE is a widespread notion that all wood will float on water, and this idea often leads to laughable errors. I know a lot of young backwoods farmers who launched a raft of green oak logs, and were as much astonished to see their craft settle quietly to the bottom of the lake as they would have been to see the leaden sinkers of their fish-lines dance lightly on the surface of the waves. The young fellows used a day's time to discover what they might have learned in a few moments by watching the chips sink when they struck the water as they flew from the skilful blows of their axes.

The stream which cuts your trail is not always provided with bridges of fallen trees. It may be a river too deep to ford and too wide to be bridged by a chance log. Of course it is a simple matter to swim, but the weather may be cold and the water still colder; besides this, you will probably be encumbered with a lot of camp equipage—your gun, rod, and camera—none of which will be improved by a plunge in the water. Or it may so happen that you are on the shores of a lake unsupplied with boats, and you have good reasons for supposing that big fish lurk in some particular spot out of reach from the shore. A thousand and one emergencies may arise when a craft of some kind will

3

be not only a great convenience, but almost a necessity.   Under these circumstances

A Logomaran

may be constructed in a very short time which can bear you and your pack safely to the desired goal (Fig. 1).

In the Rocky, Cascade, and Selkirk Mountains, the lakes and streams have their shores plentifully supplied with "whim sticks," logs of fine dry timber, which the freshets have brought down from the mountain sides and which the rocks and surging torrents have denuded of bark.   These whim sticks are of all

Fig. 2.—The notch.   Fig. 3.—Top view of logomaran.

sizes, and as sound and perfect as kiln-dried logs.   Even in the mountains of Pennsylvania, where the lumberman's axe years ago laid waste the primeval forest, where the saw-mills have devoured the second growth, the tie-hunter the third growth, the excelsior-mills and birch-beer factories the saplings, I still find good sound white pine-log whim sticks strewn along the shores of the lakes and streams, timber which is suitable for temporary rafts and logomarans.

In the North Woods, where in many localities the original forest is untouched by the devouring pulp-mills, suitable timber is not difficult to find; so let the green wood stand and select a log of dry wood from the shore where the floods or ice have deposited it. Cut it into a convenient length, and with a lever made of a good stout sapling, and a fulcrum of a stone or chunk

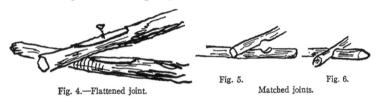

Fig. 4.—Flattened joint.   Fig. 5.   Fig. 6.
Matched joints.

of wood, pry the log from its resting-place and roll it into the shallow water. Notch the log on the upper side, as shown by Fig. 2, making a notch near each end for the cross-pieces.

The two side floats may be made of pieces split, by the aid of wooden wedges, from a large log, or composed of small whim sticks, as shown by Fig. 3.

The floats, as may be seen by reference to Figs. 1 and 3, are shorter than the middle log.

It is impracticable to give dimensions, for the reason that they are relative; the length of the middle log depends, to some extent, upon its diameter, it being evident that a thick log will support more than a thin one of the same length; consequently if your log is of small diameter, it must be longer, in order to support your weight, than will be necessary for a thicker piece of timber. The point to remember is to select a log which will support you and your pack, and then attach two side floats to balance your craft and prevent it from rolling over and dumping its load in the water.

An ordinary single shell-boat without a passenger will upset, but when the oarsman takes his seat and grasps his long spoon oars, the sweeps, resting on the water, balance the cranky craft, and it cannot upset as long as the oars are kept there. This is the principle of the logomaran, as well as that of the common catamaran. The cross-pieces should be only thick enough to be se-

Fig. 7.—The saw-buck crib.   Fig. 8.—The staked crib.

cure and long enough to prevent the log from wabbling and wetting your feet more than is necessary.

If You Have an Auger and No Nails

the craft may be fastened together with wooden pegs cut somewhat larger than the holes bored to receive them, and driven in with blows from your axe.

If you have long nails or spikes the problem is a simple one; but if you have neither auger, nails, nor spikes you must bind the joints with rope or hempen twine.

If you have neither nails, auger, nor rope, a good substitute for the latter can be made from the long,

Fibrous Inner Bark

of a dead or partly burned tree. For experiment I took some of the inner bark of a chestnut-tree which had been killed by fire and twisted it into a rope the size of a clothes-line, then I allowed two strong men to have a tug-of-war with it, and the improvised rope was stronger than the men.

How to Make a Fibre Rope

Take one end of a long, loose strand of fibres, give the other end to another person, and let both twine the ends between the fingers until the material is well twisted throughout its entire length; then bring the two ends together, and two sides of the loop thus made will twist themselves into a cord or rope half the length of the original strand.

If you nail or peg the parts, use your axe to flatten the joints by striking off a chip, as in Fig. 4.

If you must lash the joints together, cut them with log-cabin notches, as in Figs. 5 and 6.

If you have baggage to transport, make

A Dunnage Crib

by driving four stakes in cuts made near the end of the centre log and binding them with rope or fibre (Figs. 7 and 8), or by working green twigs basket-fashion around them, or make the rack saw-buck fashion, as shown by Fig. 7, and this will keep your things above water.

A couple of cleats nailed on each side of the log will be of great assistance and lessen the danger and insecurity of the footing.

A skilfully made logomaran will enable you to cross any stream with a moderate current and any small lake in moderate weather. It is not an especially dry craft, but it won't sink or upset, and will take one but a short time to knock it together.

CHAPTER II

Birth of the "Man-Friday" Catamaran—The Crusoe Raft and Chump Rafts

NOT so very many years ago I remember visiting, in company with my cousin Tom, a small lake at the headwaters of the Miami. High and precipitous cliffs surround the little body of water. So steep were the great weather-beaten rocks that it was only where the stream came tumbling down past an old mill that an accessible path then existed. Down that path Tom and I scrambled, for we knew that large bass lurked in the deep, black holes among the rocks.

We had no jointed split-bamboo rods nor fancy tackle, but the fish there in those days were not particular and seldom hesitated to bite at an angle-worm or grasshopper though the hook upon which the bait squirmed was suspended by a coarse line from a freshly cut hickory sapling.

Even now I feel the thrill of excitement and expectancy as, in imagination, my pole is bent nearly double by the frantic struggles of those "gamy" black bass. After spending the morning fishing we built a fire upon a short stretch of sandy beach, and cleaning our fish and washing them in the spring close at hand, we put them among the embers to cook.

While the fire was getting our dinner ready for us we threw off our clothes and plunged into the cool waters of the lake. Inexpert swimmers as we were at that time, the opposite shore, though apparently only a stone's throw distant, was too far off for us to reach by swimming. Many a longing and curious glance we cast toward it, however, and strong was the temptation that beset us to try the unknown depths intervening. A pair of brown ears appeared above the ferns near the water's edge, and a fox peeped at us; squirrels ran about the fallen trunks of trees or scampered up the rocks as saucily as though they understood that we could not swim well enough to reach

Fig. 8½.—The Man-Friday.

their side of the lake; and high up the face of the cliff was a dark spot which we almost knew to be the entrance to some mysterious cavern.

How we longed for a boat! But not even a raft nor a dugout could be seen anywhere upon the glassy surface of the water or along its rocky border. We nevertheless determined to explore the lake next day, even if we should have to paddle astride of a log.

The first rays of the morning sun had not reached the dark waters before my companion and I were hard at work, with axe and hatchet, chopping in twain a long log we had discovered near the mill. We had at first intended to build a raft; but gradually we evolved a sort of catamaran. The two pieces of log we sharpened at the ends for the bow; then we rolled the logs down upon the beach, and while I went into the thicket to chop down some saplings my companion borrowed an auger from the miller. We next placed the logs about three feet apart, and marking the points where we intended to put the cross-pieces, we cut notches there; then we placed the saplings across, fitting them into these notches. To hold them securely we bored holes down through the sapling cross-pieces into the logs; with the hatchet we hammered wooden pegs into these holes. For the seat we used the half of a section of log, the flat side fitting into places cut for that purpose. All that remained to be done now was to make a seat in the stern and a pair of rowlocks. At a proper distance from the oarsman's seat we bored two holes for a couple of forked sticks, which answered admirably for rowlocks; across the stern we fastened another piece of log similar to that used for the oarsman's seat (Fig. 8½). With the help of a man from the mill our craft was launched; and with a pair of oars made of old pine boards we rowed off, leaving the miller waving his hat.

Our catamaran was not so light as a row-boat, but it floated, and we could propel it with the oars, and, best of all, it was our own invention and made with our own hands. We called it a "Man-Friday," and by its means we explored every nook in the length and breadth of the lake; and ever afterward when we wanted a boat we knew a simple and inexpensive way to make one—and a safe one, too.

The Crusoe Raft

is another rustic craft, but it is of more ambitious dimensions than the "Man-Friday." Instead of being able to float only one or two passengers, the "Crusoe," if properly built, ought to accommodate a considerable party of raftsmen. Of course the purpose for which the raft is to be used, and the number of the crew that is expected to man it, must be taken into consideration when deciding upon the dimensions of the proposed craft.

All the tools that are necessary for the construction of a good stout raft are an axe, an auger, and a hatchet, with some strong arms to wield them.

The building material can be gathered from any driftwood heap on lake or stream.

For a moderate-sized raft collect six or seven logs, the longest not being over sixteen feet in length nor more than a foot in diameter; the logs must be tolerably straight. Pick out the longest and biggest for the centre, sharpen one end, roll the log into the water, and there secure it.

Select two logs as nearly alike as possible, to lie one at each side of the centre log. Measure the centre log, and make the

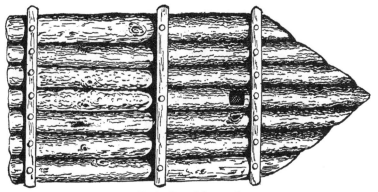

Fig. 9.—Plan of Crusoe raft.

point of each side log, not at its own centre, but at that side of it which will lie against the middle log, so that this side point shall terminate where the pointing of the middle log begins (see Fig. 9).

After all the logs needed have been trimmed and sharpened in the manner just described, roll them into the water and arrange them in order (Fig. 9). Fasten them together with "cross-strips," boring holes through the strips to correspond with holes bored into the logs lying beneath, and through these holes drive wooden pegs. The pegs should be a trifle larger than the holes; the water will cause the pegs to swell, and they will hold much more firmly than iron nails.

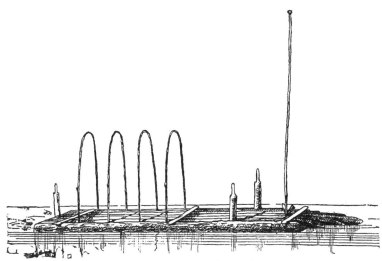

Fig. 10.—Skeleton of Crusoe raft.

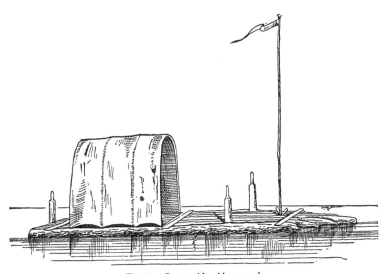

Fig. 11.—Crusoe with cabin covered.

The skeleton of the cabin can be made of saplings; such as are used for hoop-poles are the best.

These are each bent into an arch, and the ends are thrust into holes bored for that purpose. Over this hooping a piece of canvas is stretched, after the manner of old-fashioned country wagons (Figs. 10 and 11).

Erect a "jack-staff," to be used as a flag-pole or a mast to rig a square sail on.

A stout stick should be erected at the stern, and a similar one upon each side of the raft near the bow; these sticks, when

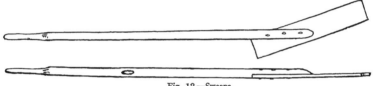

Fig. 12.—Sweeps.

their ends are made smaller, as shown in the illustration (Fig. 10), serve as rowlocks.

For oars use "sweeps"—long poles, each with a piece of board for a blade fastened at one end (Fig. 12).

Holes must be bored through the poles of the sweeps about three feet from the handle, to slip over the pegs used as rowlocks, as described above. These pegs should be high enough to allow the oarsman to stand while using the sweeps.

A flat stone or earth box placed at the bow will serve as a fireplace.

If the cracks between the logs under the cabin are filled up to prevent the water splashing through, and the cabin is floored with cross-sticks, a most comfortable bed at night can be made of hay, by heaping it under the canvas cover in sufficient quantities.

The Crusoe raft has this great advantage over all boats: you may take a long trip down the river, allowing the current to bear you along, using the sweeps only to assist the man at the helm (rear sweep); then, after your excursion is finished you may

abandon your raft and return by steam-boat or train. A very
useful thing to the swimmers, when they are skylarking in the
water, is

The Chump's Raft

Its construction is simple. Four boards, each about six feet
long, are nailed together in the form of a square, with the ends
of the boards protruding, like the figure drawn upon a school-
boy's slate for the game of "Tit, tat, toe" (Fig. 13).

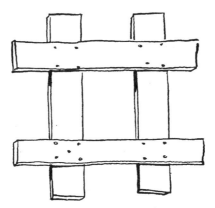

Fig. 13.—The chump's raft.

All nail-points must be knocked off and the heads hammered
home, to prevent serious scratches and wounds on the bather's
body when he clambers over the raft or slips off in an attempt to
do so (Fig. 14).

Beginners get in the middle hole, and there, with a support
within reach all around them, they can venture with compara-
tive safety in deep water.

The raft, which I built as a model fifteen years ago, is still in
use at my summer camp, where scores of young people have
used it with a success proved by their present skill as swimmers. But many camps are located in a section of the country

where boards are as scarce as boarding-houses, but where timber, in its rough state, exists in abundance. The campers in such locations can make

A Chump's Raft of Logs

Such a float consists of two dried logs fastened together at each end by cross-slabs, so as to form a rude catamaran. These rafts can be towed through deep water by a canoe or row-boat, with

Fig. 14.—A beginner in a chump's raft.

the tenderfoot securely swung in a sling between the logs, where he may practice the hand-and-foot movement with a sense of security which only the certainty that he is surrounded by a wooden life-preserver will give him. Fig. 15 shows a top view of the new chump's raft. In Fig. 16 the two logs are connected fore and aft by cross-slabs; two more upright slabs are nailed securely to the side of the logs; notches having been cut in the top ends of these slabs, a stout cross-piece is securely nailed to them and the towel or rope sling suspended from the middle of the cross-piece. In regard to the dimensions of the raft it is only necessary to say that it should be wide and long enough to allow free movement of the arms and legs of the pupil who is suspended between the logs. In almost every wilderness stream there can

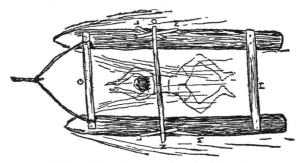

Fig. 15.—Looking down on a chump's raft in motion.

be found piles of driftwood on the shore where one may select good, dried, well-seasoned pine or spruce logs from which to make rafts. If such heaps of driftwood are not within reach, look for some standing dead timber and select that which is of sufficient dimensions to support a swimmer, and be careful that it is not hollow or rotten in the core. Rotten wood will soon become

Fig. 16.—Side view of chump's log raft.

water-logged and heavy. Fig. 17 shows the position of the swimmer supported by the chump's sling. If your raft has a tendency to work so that one log pulls ahead of the other, it may be braced by cross-pieces, such as are shown at J and K in Fig. 18. This figure also shows supports for a suspension pole made

by nailing two sticks to each side and allowing the ends to cross
so as to form a crotch in which the supporting rod rests and to
which it is securely fastened by nails, or by being bound there by
a piece of rope, as in A, Fig. 19. B, Fig. 19, shows the crotch

Fig. 17.—Learning to swim by aid of a chump sling.

Fig. 19.—Details of saw-
buck supports.

made by resting L in a fork on the M stick and then nailing or
binding it in place. C, Fig. 19, shows the two sticks, L and M,
joined by notches cut log-cabin fashion before they are nailed
in place.

Although many summers have rolled around since the author
first made his advent on this beautiful earth, he still feels the call
of the bathing pool, the charm of the spring-board, almost as
keenly as he did when he was wont to swim in Blue Hole at
Yellow Springs, Ohio, or dive from the log rafts into the Ohio
River, or slide down the "slippery" made in the steep muddy
banks of the Licking River, Kentucky.

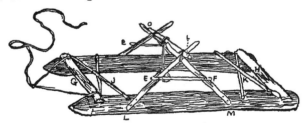

Fig. 18.—Another way to rig a chump.

CHAPTER III

A RAFT THAT WILL SAIL

The Raft is Just the Thing for Camp Life—Pleasurable Occupation for a Camping Party Where Wood is Plentiful—You Will Need Axes and Hatchets and a Few Other Civilized Implements

FIRST we will select two pine logs of equal length, and, while the water is heating for our coffee, we will sharpen the butt, or larger end, of the logs on one side with the axe, making a "chisel edge," as shown in Fig. 20. This gives us an appetite for breakfast and makes the big fish in the lake, as they jump above the water, cast anxious looks toward our camp.

Breakfast finished, we will cut some cross-pieces to join our two logs together, and at equal distances apart we will bore holes through the cross-pieces for peg-holes (Figs. 21, 22, and 23). While one of the party is fashioning a number of pegs, each with a groove in one side, like those shown in Fig. 24, the others will roll the logs into the water and secure them in a shallow spot.

Shoes and stockings must be removed, for most of the work is now to be done in the water. Of course, it would be much easier done on land, but the raft will be very heavy and could never be launched unless under the most favorable circumstances. It is better to build the craft in the element which is to be its home.

Cut two long saplings for braces, and after separating the logs the proper distance for your cross-pieces to fit, nail your braces in position, as represented by Fig. 20.

This holds the logs steady, and we may now lay the two cross-pieces in position, and mark the points on the logs carefully

18

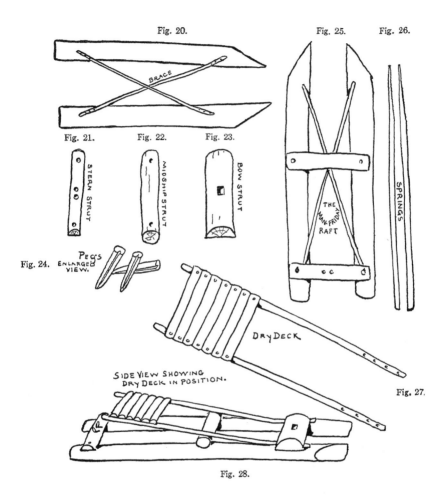

Fig. 20.
Fig. 25. Fig. 26.
Fig. 21. Fig. 22. Fig. 23.

BRACE

STERN STRUT
MIDSHIP STRUT
BOW STRUT

SPRINGS

THE MAN-FRIDAY RAFT

Fig. 24. PEGS ENLARGED VIEW.

DRY DECK

Fig. 27.

SIDE VIEW SHOWING DRY DECK IN POSITION.

Fig. 28.

PARTS OF MAN-FRIDAY SAILING-RAFT.

Fig. 20.—Logs in place with braces.   Figs. 21, 22, and 23.—Struts.   Fig. 24.—Pegs.   Fig. 25.—
Raft with middle and stern strut in place.   Fig. 26.—Springs for dry deck.   Fig. 27.—Dry deck.
Fig. 28.—Dry deck in place.

where the holes are to be bored to correspond with the ones in the cross-pieces. Bore the holes in one log first; make the holes deep enough and then fill them with water, after which drive the pegs through the ends of the cross-pieces and into the log. The grooves in the pegs (Fig. 24) will allow the water to escape from the holes and the water will cause the peg to swell and tighten its hold on the log and cross-pieces.

Now bore holes in the other log under those in the cross-pieces and fill them with water before driving the pegs home, as you did in the first instance. Fig. 25 is a Man-Friday raft.

The Deck

Before placing the bow in position we must go ashore and make a dry deck. Selecting for the springs two long green ash or hickory poles, trim the ends off flat on one side, as shown by Fig. 26. This flat side is the bottom, so roll them over, with the flat side toward the ground, and if you can find no planks or barrel staves for a deck, split in half a number of small logs and peg or nail them on the top side of the springs, as in Fig. 27.

Now all hands must turn out and carry the deck down to the raft and place it in position, with the flattened sides of the springs resting on top of the logs at the bow. Prop it up in this position, and then bore holes through the springs into the logs and peg the springs down. Over the flat ends place the heavy bow cross-piece, bore the peg-holes, and fasten it in position (Fig. 28).

In the centre of the bow cross-piece bore several holes close together and chip out the wood between to make a hole, as square a one as possible, for the mast to fit or "step" in. With the wood from a packing-box or a slab from a log make the bench for the mast.

Bore a hole through the bench a trifle astern of the step, or hole, for the mast below. It will cause the mast to "rake" a little "aft." You have done a big day's work, but a couple of days ought to be sufficient time to finish the craft.

The Sail

Turn over the raw edges of the old sail-cloth and stitch them down, as in Fig. 29—that is, if you have the needle and thread for the purpose; if not, trim the cloth to the proper form and two

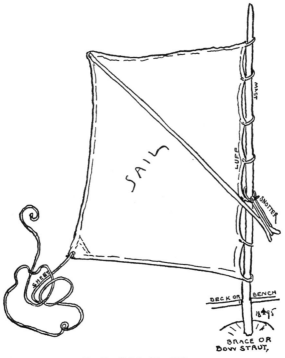

Fig. 29.—Sail for Man-Friday.

inches from the luff (the side next to the mast). Cut a number of holes; these should be stitched like button-holes, if possible, but if the sail-cloth is tough and we have no needle, we shall have to let them go unstitched. A small loop of rope must be sewed or fastened in some other manner very securely to each corner of the sail.

From spruce pine or an old fishing-pole make a sprit, and of a good, straight piece of pine manufacture your mast somewhat longer than the luff of the sail (Fig. 29).

Through the eyelets lace the luff of the sail to the mast, so that its lower edge will clear the dry deck by about a foot.

Fig. 30.—Scudding before the wind.

Through the hole made for the purpose in the bench (Fig. 30) thrust the mast into the step, or socket, that we have cut in the bow cross-piece.   Tie to the loop at the bottom corner of the sail a strong line about twelve feet long for a sheet with which to control the sail.

Trim the upper end of the sprit to fit in the loop at the upper outer corner of the sail, and make a notch in the lower end to fit in the loop of the line called the "snotter."

Now, as you can readily see, when the sprit is pushed diagonally upward the sail is spread; to hold it in place make a loop of line for a "snotter" and attach the loop to the mast, as in Figs. 29 and 30. Fit the loop in the notch in the lower end of the sprit, and the sail is set.

The Keelig

We need anchors, one for the bow and one for the stern. It takes little time to make them, as you only need a forked stick,

Fig. 31. Fig. 32. Fig. 33. Fig. 34. Fig. 37.

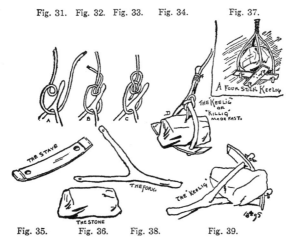

Fig. 35. Fig. 36. Fig. 38. Fig. 39.

a stone, and a piece of plank, or, better still, a barrel stave. Figs. 35 to 39 show how this is made. Down East the fishermen use the "keelig" in preference to any other anchor.

Make fast your lines to the "keelig" thus: Take the end of the rope in your right hand and the standing part (which is the part leading from the boat) in your left hand and form the loop (A, Fig. 31).

Then with the left hand curve the cable from you, bringing the end through the loop, as in B, Fig. 32; then lead it around and down, as in C, Fig. 33.

Draw it tight, as in D, Fig. 34, and you have the good, old-fashioned knot, called by sailors the "bow-line."

To make it look neat and shipshape you may take a piece of string and bind the standing part to the shaft of your anchor or keelig—keelek—killick—killeck—kelleck—kellock—killock, etc., as you may choose to spell it.

A paddle to steer with and two pegs in the stern cross-piece to rest it in complete the craft; and now the big bass had better use due caution, because our lines will reach their haunts, and we are after them!

CHAPTER IV

CANOES

The Advantages of a Canoe—How to Make the Slab Canoe and the Dugout—How to Make a Siwash and a White Man's Dugout

THERE are many small freak crafts invented each year, but none of them has any probabilities of being popularly used as substitutes for the old models.

Folding canoes, as a rule, are cranky, but the writer has found them most convenient when it was necessary to transport them long distances overland. They are not, however, the safest of crafts; necessarily they lack the buoyant wooden frame and lining of the ordinary canvas canoe, which enables it to float even when filled with water.

The author owes his life to the floating properties of his canvas canoe. On one occasion when it upset in a driving easterly storm the wind was off shore, and any attempt upon the canoeist's part to swim toward shore would have caused him to have been suffocated by the tops of the waves which the wind cut off, driving the water with stinging force into his face so constantly that, in order to breathe at all, he had to face the other way. He was at length rescued by a steamer, losing nothing but the sails and his shoes. Nevertheless, the same storm which capsized his little craft upset several larger boats and tore the sails from others.

The advantages of a good canoe are many for the young navigators: they can launch their own craft, pick it up when occasion demands and carry it overland. It is safe in experienced hands in any weather which is fit for out-door amusement. When you are "paddling your own canoe" you are facing to the front and can see what is ahead of you, which is much safer and more pleasant than travelling backward, like a crawfish.

The advance-guard of modern civilization is the lumberman, and following close on his heels comes the all-devouring saw-mill. This fierce creature has an abnormal appetite for logs,

THE SLAB

Fig. 40.

and it keeps an army of men, boys, and horses busy in supplying it with food. While it supplies us with lumber for the carpenter, builder, and cabinet-maker, it at the same time, in the most shameful way, fills the trout streams and rivers with great masses of sawdust, which kills and drives away the fish. But near the saw-mill there is always to be found material for a

Slab Canoe

which consists simply of one of those long slabs, the first cut from some giant log (Fig. 43).

These slabs are burned or thrown away by the mill-owners, and hence cost nothing; and as the saw-mill is in advance of population, you are most likely to run across one on a hunting or fishing trip.

Near one end, and on the flat side of the slab (Fig. 40), bore four holes, into which drive the four legs of a stool made of a section of a smaller slab (Fig. 41), and your boat is ready to launch. From a piece of board make a double or single paddle (Fig. 42), and you are equipped for a voyage. An old gentleman, who in his boyhood days on the frontier frequently used this simple style of canoe, says that the speed it makes will compare favorably with that of many a more pretentious vessel. See Fig. 43 for furnished boat.

The Dugout

Although not quite as delicate in model or construction as the graceful birch-bark canoe, the "dugout" of the Indians is a

Fig. 41.

most wonderful piece of work, when we consider that it is carved from the solid trunk of a giant tree with the crudest of tools.

Few people now living have enjoyed the opportunity of seeing one built by the Indians, and, as the author is not numbered among that select few, he considers it a privilege to be able to quote the following interesting account given by Mr. J. H. Mallett, of Helena.

How to Build a Siwash Canoe

"While visiting one of the small towns along Puget Sound, I was greatly interested in the way the Indians built their canoes.

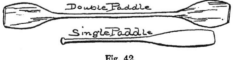

Fig. 42.

It is really wonderful how these native people can, with the crudest means and with a few days' work, convert an unwieldy log into a trim and pretty canoe.

"One Monday morning I saw a man building a fire at the base of a large cedar-tree, and he told me that this was the first step in the construction of a canoe that he intended to use upon the following Saturday. He kept the fire burning merrily all that day and far into the night, when a wind came up and completed

Fig. 43.—Slab canoe.

the downfall of the monarch of the forest. The next day the man arose betimes, and, borrowing a cross-cut saw from a logger, cut the trunk of the tree in twain at a point some fifteen feet from where it had broken off, and then with a dull hatchet he hacked away until the log had assumed the shape of the desired canoe. In this work he was helped by his wife. The old fellow then built a fire on the upper part of the log, guiding the course of the fire with daubs of clay, and in due course of time the interior of the canoe had been burned out. Half a day's work with the hatchet rendered the inside smooth and shapely.

"The canoe was now, I thought, complete, though it appeared to be dangerously narrow of beam. This the Indian soon remedied. He filled the shell two-thirds full of water, and into the fluid he dropped half a dozen stones that had been heating in the fire for nearly a day. The water at once attained a boiling point, and so softened the wood that the man and woman were enabled to draw out the sides and thus supply the necessary breadth of beam. Thwarts and slats were then placed in the canoe and the water and stones thrown out. When the steamed wood began to cool and contract, the thwarts held it

Fig. 44.—The dugout.

back, and the sides held the thwarts, and there the canoe was complete, without a nail, joint, or crevice, for it was made of one piece of wood. The Siwash did not complete it as soon as he had promised, but it only took him eight days."

In the North-eastern part of our country, before the advent of the canvas canoe, beautiful and light birch-bark craft were used by the Indians, the voyagers, trappers, and white woodsmen. But in the South and in the North-west, the dugout takes the place of the birch-bark. Among the North-western Indians the dugouts are made from the trunks of immense cedar-trees and built with high, ornamental bows, which are brilliantly decorated with paint. On the eastern shore of Maryland and Virginia the dugout is made into a sail-boat called the buck-eye,

or bug-eye.   But all through the Southern States, from the Ohio
River to the Gulf of Mexico and in Mexico, the dugout is made
of a hollowed log after the manner of an ordinary horse trough,
and often it is as crude as the latter, but it can be made almost
as beautiful and graceful as a birch-bark canoe.

How to Make a White Man's Dugout Canoe

To make one of these dugout canoes one must be big and
strong enough to wield an axe, but if the readers are too young

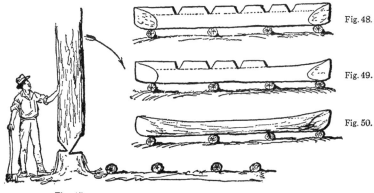

Fig. 48.

Fig. 49.

Fig. 50.

Fig. 45.

for this work, they are none too young to know how to make
one, and their big brothers and father can do the work.   Since
the dugout occupies an important position in the history of our
country, every boy scout should know how it is made.

Fig. 44 shows one of these canoes afloat; Fig. 45 shows a tall,
straight tree suitable for our purpose, and it also shows how the
tree is cut and the arrangement of the kerfs, or two notches, so that
it will fall in the direction of the arrow in the diagram.   You will
notice along the ground are shown the ends of a number of small
logs.   These are the skids, or rollers, upon which the log will rest
when the tree is cut and felled.   The tree will fall in the direction

in which the arrow is pointed if there is no wind. If you have never cut down a tree, be careful to take some lessons of a good woodsman before you attempt it.

When the log is trimmed off at both ends like Fig. 46, flatten the upper side with the axe. This is for the bottom of the canoe; the flat part should be about a foot and a half wide to extend

Fig. 46.

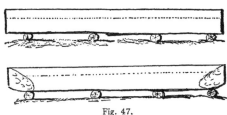

Fig. 47.

from end to end of the log. Now, with some poles for pryers, turn your log over so that it will rest with the flat bottom on the skids, as in Fig. 46.

Next take a chalk-line and fasten it at the two ends of the log, as shown by the dotted line in Figs. 46, 47, 48, 49.

Snap the line so that it will make a straight mark as shown by the dotted line; then trim off the two ends for the bow and stern, as shown in Fig. 47. Next cut notches down to the dotted line, as illustrated in Fig. 48; then cut away from the bow down to the first notch, making a curved line, as shown in Fig. 49 (which is cut to second notch). Do the same with the stern, making duplicates of the bow and stern. The spaces between the notches amidships may now be split off by striking your axe along the chalk-line and then carefully driving in wooden wedges. When this is all done you will have Fig. 50. You can now turn the log over and trim off the edges of the bow and stern so that they will slope, as shown in Fig. 44, in a rounded curve; after which roll the canoe back again upon its bottom and with an adze and axe hollow out the inside, leaving some solid wood at both bow and stern—not that you need the wood for strength, but to save labor.   When you have decided upon the thickness of the sides of your canoe, take some small, pointed instrument, like an awl, for instance, and make holes with it to the required depth at intervals along the sides and bottom of the canoe.   Then take some small sticks (as long as the canoe sides are to be thick), make them to fit the holes, blacken their ends, and drive them into the holes.

As soon as you see one from the inside, you will know that you have made the shell thin enough.   Use a jack-plane to smooth it off inside and out; then build a big fire and heat some stones. Next fill the canoe with water and keep dumping the hot stones in the water until the latter is almost or quite to boiling point. The hot water will soften the wood so that the sides will become flexible, and you can then fit in some braces at the bow, stern, and centre of the canoe.   Make the centre brace or seat some inches wider than the log, so that when it is forced in place it will spread the canoe in the middle.

CHAPTER V

In making canoes the Indians used birch bark for the cover, rock maple for the cross-bars, and white cedar for the rest of the frame. We will substitute canvas for the birch bark and any old wood that we can for the rock maple and the white cedar. *Real woodcraft is best displayed in the ability to use the material at hand.*

David Abercrombie, the outfitter, some time ago presented Andrew J. Stone, the Arctic explorer and mighty hunter, with a small piece of light, water-proof cloth to use as a shelter tent in bad weather. But Stone, like the hunter that he was, slept unprotected on the mountain side in the sleet and driving storms, and used the water-proof cloth to protect the rare specimens he had shot. One day a large, rapid torrent lay in his path; there was no lumber large enough with which to build a raft, and the only wood for miles around was small willow bushes growing along the river bank. At his command, his three Indians made a canoe frame of willow sticks, tied together with bits of cloth and string. Stone set this frame in the middle of his water-proof cloth, tied the cloth over the frame with other pieces of string, and using only small clubs for paddles, he and his men crossed the raging torrent in this makeshift, which was loaded with their guns, camera, and specimens that he had shot on the trip.

After reading the above there is no doubt the reader will be able to build a war canoe with barrel-hoop ribs and lattice-work slats. In the writer's studio is a long piece of maple, one and one-half inches wide and one-quarter inch thick, which was left by the workmen when they put down a hard-wood floor. If you can get some similar strips, either of oak, maple, or birch, from the dealers in flooring material, they will not be expensive and will make splendid gunwales for your proposed canoe. There should be four such strips. The hard-wood used for flooring splits easily, and holes should be bored for the nails or screws to prevent cracking the wood when the nails or screws are driven home. Fig. 51 shows the framework (side view) of the canoe; Fig. 52 shows an end view of the same canoe; Fig. 53 shows the middle section, and Fig. 54 shows the form of the bow and stern sections. This boat may be built any length you wish, and so that you may get the proper proportions, the diagrams from one to five are marked off in equal divisions. To make patterns of the moulds, Figs. 53 and 54, take a large piece of manila paper, divide it up into the same number of squares as the diagram, make the squares any size you may decide upon, and then trace the line, 1–H–10, as it is in the diagrams. This will give you the patterns of the two moulds (Figs. 53 and 54). While you are looking at these figures, it may be well to call your attention to the way bow and stern pieces are made. In Fig. 63 the pieces Y and X are made from pieces of a packing-box, notched and nailed together with a top piece, U, and a brace, V.

The other end of the same canoe is, as you may see, strengthened and protected by having a barrel-hoop tacked over the stem-pieces, Y, X, U. In Fig. 64 we use different material; here the stem-piece is made of a broken bicycle rim, U, braced by the pieces of packing-box, Y, V, and W. The left-hand end of Fig. 64 is made with pieces of head of a barrel, X and U. The bottom of the stem-piece Y is made of the piece of a packing box. The two braces V are parts of the barrel-stave. Fig. 60 shows the common form of the bow of a canoe. The stem-pieces

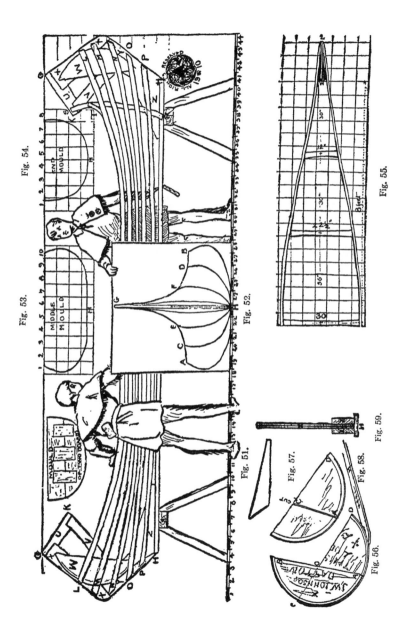

Fig. 53.

Fig. 54.

Fig. 55.

Fig. 52.

Fig. 51.

Fig. 57.

Fig. 58.

Fig. 59.

Fig. 56.

X, Y are made of the parts of the head of a barrel, as shown in Fig. 62. To make a stem from a barrel-head, nail the two pieces X and Y, Fig. 56, together as shown in this particular diagram. Now take another piece of barrel-head, Fig. 57, and saw off a piece, A', D', C', so that it will fit neatly over A, C, D, on Fig. 56. Nail this securely in place, and then in the same manner cut another piece to fit over the part E, C, B, and nail that in place. Use small nails, but let them be long enough so that you may clinch them by holding an axe or an iron against the head while you hammer the protruding points down, or drive the nail a little on the bias and holding the axe or iron on the side it is to come through and let it strike the nail as it comes out and it will clinch itself. To fasten the stem-piece to the keel use two pieces of packing-box or board, cut in the form of Fig. 58, and nail these securely to the bow-piece as in Z, in Fig. 60. Then from the bottom side of the keel H, nail the keel-pieces firmly to the keel as in Fig. 61. Also drive some nails from Z to the top down to the keel, as shown by the dotted lines in Fig. 60. The end view, Fig. 59, shows how the two Z pieces hug and support the stem-piece on the keel H. Fig. 55 shows a half of the top view of the canoe gunwales; the dimensions, marked in feet and inches, are taken from an Indian birch-bark canoe. You see by the diagram that it is eight feet from the centre of the middle cross-piece to the end of the big opening at the bow. It is also three feet from the centre of the middle cross-piece to the next cross-piece, and thirty inches from the centre of that cross-piece to the bow cross-piece, which is just thirty inches from the eight-foot mark. The middle cross-piece in a canoe of these dimensions is seven-eighths of an inch thick, and thirty inches long between the gunwales; the next cross-piece is three-quarters of an inch thick and twenty-two and one-half inches long. The next one is half an inch wide, two inches thick and twelve inches between the gunwales. These cross-pieces can be made of the staves of a barrel. Of course, this would be a canoe of sixteen feet inside measurement, not counting the flattened part of the bow and stern. Now, then, to build the canoe. First take the keel-piece, H, which is in this case a piece of board about six inches wide and only thick enough to be moderately stiff. Lay the keel on any level surface and put the stem-pieces on as already described, using packing-box for X, U, V, Y, and Z, and

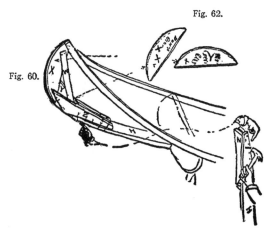

Fig. 62.

Fig. 60.

Fig. 61.

Conventional bow, but made of barrel-heads.

bracing them with a piece of packing-box on each side, marked W in diagram (Fig. 51). Then make three moulds, one for the centre (Fig. 53), and two more for the bow and stern (Fig. 54). Notch the bottom of these moulds to fit the keel and with wire nails make them fast to the keel, leaving the ends of the nails protruding far enough to be easily withdrawn when you wish to remove the moulds. In nailing the laths to the moulds (Fig. 51) leave the heads of the nails also protruding so that they may be removed. Place the moulds in position, with the middle one in the exact centre, and the two ends located like those in Figs. 63 and 64. Place and nail gunwale, L, on as in Fig. 51, tacking it to the bow and stern and bending it around to fit the moulds;

tack the lattice slats M, N, O, P on to the bow, stern, and moulds, as shown in Fig. 51.

If your barrel-hoops are stiff and liable to break while bending and unbending, let them soak a couple of days in a tub of water, then before fitting them to the form of the canoe make them more pliable by pouring hot water on them. The barrel-hoop S, R, at the bow of the canoe, is nailed to the top-piece U, to the inside of the slats L, M, N, O, P, and to the outside of H. The next three ribs on each side are treated in the same manner; repeat this at the other end of the canoe and nail the intervening ribs to the top of H and to the inside of the slats, following the model of the boat. Put the ribs about four inches apart and clinch the nails as already described.

In the diagrams there is no temporary support for the canoe frame except the wooden horses, as in Fig. 51. These supports have been purposely omitted in the drawing, as it is desirable to keep it as simple as possible. Some temporary support will be necessary to hold the bow and stern-piece in Fig. 51. These supports can be nailed or screwed temporarily to the canoe frame so as to hold it rigid while you are at work on it.

After the ribs are all in place and the framework completed, turn the canoe upside down upon the wooden horses—for a canoe as large as the one in the first diagram you will need three horses, one at each end and one in the middle. For a canoe of the dimensions marked in Fig. 55, that is, sixteen feet inside measurement, you would need about seven yards of ten-ounce cotton canvas, of sufficient width to reach up over the sides of your canoe. Take a tape-measure or a piece of ordinary tape or a long strip of manila paper and measure around the bottom of the boat at its widest part in the middle from one gunwale (top of side) to the other, and see that your cloth is fully as wide as your measurement. Fold the canvas lengthwise so as to find its exact centre and crease it. With two or three tacks fasten the cloth at its centre line (the crease) to the stem-piece of the canoe. Stretch the canvas the length of the boat with the crease of centre-line along the centre of the keel, pull it as taut as may be and again tack the centre line to the stem at this end of the craft. If this has been done carefully the cloth will hang an equal length over each side of the canoe. Now begin amidships and drive tacks about two inches apart along the gunwale, say an inch below the top surface. After having tacked it for about two feet, go to the other side of

Fig. 63.

Fig. 64.
High bows framework made of packing-box and barrel-heads.

the boat, pull the cloth taut and in the same manner tack about three feet. Continue this process first one side and then the other until finished. While stretching the cloth knead it with the hand and fingers so as to thicken or "full" it where it would otherwise wrinkle; by doing this carefully it is possible to stretch the canvas over the frame without the necessity of cutting it. The cloth that extends beyond the frame may be brought over the gunwale and tacked along the inside. Use four-ounce tinned or copper tacks. The canvas is now stretched on every part except on the high, rolling bow and stern. With a pair of shears slit the canvas from the outer edge of the bow and stern within a half inch of the ends of the keel.

Fold the right-hand flap thus made at the left-hand end around the bow and stern and, drawing tight, tack it down, then fold the left-hand flap over the right-hand side and tack it in a similar manner, trimming off the remaining cloth neatly. The five braces, three of which are shown in Fig. 55, may be nailed to the gunwales of the canoe, as the temporary moulds are removed. The braces should be so notched that the top ends of the braces will fit over the top edge of the gunwale and their lower edges will fit against the sides. Give the boat at least three good coats of paint and nail the two extra gunwale strips on the outside of the canvas for guards.

When it is dry and the boat is launched you may startle the onlookers and make the echoes ring with:

"Wo-ach! wo-ach! Ha-ha-ha-hack—wo-ach!" which is said to be the identical war cry with which the Indians greeted the landing of our Pilgrim Fathers.

The reader must not suppose that barrel-hoops are the best material for ribs; they are but a makeshift, and although good-looking, servicable canoes have been built of this material from the foregoing descriptions, better ones may be made by using better material, such, for instance, as is described in the making of the birch-bark canoe.

Old Shells

Where there are oarsmen and boat-clubs, there you will find beautiful shell boats of paper or cedar, shaped like darning-needles, so slight in structure that a child can knock a hole in them, and yet very seaworthy boats for those who understand how to handle them. The expensive material and skilled labor necessary to build a racing shell puts the price of one so high that few boys can afford to buy one; but where new shells are to be found there are also old ones, and when they are too old to sell they are thrown away. Many an old shell rots on the meadows near the boat-houses or rests among the rafters forgotten and unused, which with a little work would make a boat capable of furnishing no end of fun to a boy.

Checks or Cracks

can be pasted over with common manila wrapping-paper by first covering the crack with a coat of paint, or, better still, of varnish, then fitting the paper smoothly over the spot and varnishing the paper. Give the paper several coats of varnish, allowing it to dry after each application, and the paper will become impervious to water. The deck of a shell is made of thin muslin or paper, treated with a liberal coat of varnish, and can be patched with similar material. There are always plenty of slightly damaged oars which have been discarded by the oarsmen. The use of a saw and jack-knife in the hands of a smart boy can transform these wrecks into serviceable oars for his patched-up old shell, and if the work is neatly done, the boy will be the proud owner of a real shell boat, and the envy of his comrades.

The Cause of Upsets

A single shell that is very cranky with a man in it is comparatively steady when a small boy occupies the seat. Put on your bathing clothes when you wish to try a shell, so that you may be ready for the inevitable upset. Every one knows, when he looks at one of these long, narrow boats, that as long as the oars are held extended *on the water* it cannot upset. But, in spite of that knowledge, every one, when he first gets into a shell, endeavors to balance himself by *lifting the oars*, and, of course, goes over in a jiffy.

The Delights of a Shell

It is an error to suppose that the frail-looking, needle-like boat is only fit for racing purposes. For a day on the water, in calm weather, there is, perhaps, nothing more enjoyable than a single shell. The exertion required to send it on its way is so slight, and the speed so great, that many miles can be covered with small fatigue. Upon referring to the log-book of the Nereus Club, where the distances are all taken from the United States

chart, the author finds that twenty and thirty miles are not un-
common records for single-shell rows.

During the fifteen or sixteen seasons that the author has devoted his spare time to the sport he has often planned a heavy
cruising shell, but owing to the expense of having such a boat
built he has used the ordinary racing boat, and found it remark-
ably well adapted for such purposes.   Often he has been caught
miles away from home in a blow, and only once does he remember of being compelled to seek assistance.

He was on a lee shore and the waves were so high that after
once being swamped he was unable to launch his boat again,
for it would fill before he could embark.   So a heavy rowboat
and a coachman were borrowed from a gentleman living on the
bay, and while the author rowed, the coachman towed the little
craft back to the creek where the Nereus club-house is situated.

In the creek, however, the water was calmer, and rather than
stand the jeers of his comrades, the writer embarked in his shell
and rowed up to the boat-house float.   He was very wet and his
boat was full of water, but to the inquiry of "Rough out in the
bay?" he confined himself to the simple answer—"Yes."   Then
dumping the water from his shell and placing it upon the rack.
he put on his dry clothes and walked home, none the worse for
the accident.

After ordinary skill and confidence are acquired it is really
astonishing what feats can be accomplished in a frail racing boat.

It is not difficult to

Stand Upright In a Shell

if you first take one of your long stockings and tie the handles
of your oars together where they cross each other in front of you.
The ends will work slightly and the blades will keep their positions
on the water, acting as two long balances.   Now slide your seat
as far forward as it will go, slip your feet from the straps and grasp
the staps with your hand, moving the feet back to a comfortable
position.   When all ready raise yourself by pulling on the foot

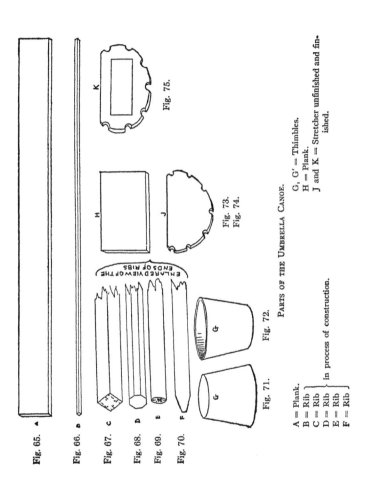

Fig. 65.

Fig. 66.

Fig. 67.

Fig. 68.

Fig. 69.

Fig. 70.

ENLARGED VIEW OF THE ENDS OF RIBS

Fig. 71.

Fig. 72.

Fig. 73.
Fig. 74.

K

Fig. 75.

PARTS OF THE UMBRELLA CANOE.

A = Plank.
B = Rib
C = Rib
D = Rib } in process of construction.
E = Rib
F = Rib

G, G' = Thimbles.
H = Plank.
J and K = Stretcher unfinished and fin-
            ished.

strap, and with ordinary care you can stand upright in the needle-shaped boat, an apparently impossible thing to do when you look at the narrow craft.

How to Land Where There Is No Float

When for any reason you wish to land where there is no float, row into shallow water and put one foot overboard until it touches bottom. Then follow with the other foot, rise, and you are standing astride of your boat.

How to Embark Where There Is No Float

Wade out and slide the shell between your extended legs until the seat is underneath you. Sit down, and, with the feet still in the water, grasp your oars. With these in your hands it is an easy task to balance the boat until you can lift your feet into it.

Ozias Dodge's Umbrella Canoe

Mr. Dodge is a Yale man, an artist, and an enthusiastic canoeist. The prow of his little craft has ploughed its way through the waters of many picturesque streams in this country and Europe, by the river-side, under the walls of ruined castles, where the iron-clad warriors once built their camp-fires, and near pretty villages, where people dress as if they were at a fancy-dress ball

When a young man like Mr. Dodge says that he has built a folding canoe that is not hard to construct, is inexpensive and practical, there can be little doubt that such a boat is not only what is claimed for it by its inventor, but that it is a novelty in its line, and such is undoubtedly the case with the umbrella canoe.

How the Canoe Was Built

The artist first secured a white-ash plank (A, Fig. 65), free from knots and blemishes of all kinds. The plank was one inch thick and about twelve feet long. At the mill he had this sawed into eight strips one inch wide, one inch thick, and twelve feet long (B and C, Figs. 66 and 67). Then he planed off the square edges of each stick until they were all octagonal in form, and looked like so many great lead-pencils (D, Fig. 68).

Mr. Dodge claims that, after you have reduced the ash poles to this octagonal form, it is an easy matter to whittle them with

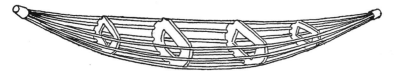

Fig. 76.—Frame of umbrella canoe.

your pocket-knife or a draw-knife, and by taking off all the angles of the sticks make them cylindrical in form (E, Fig. 69); then smooth them off nicely with sand-paper, so that each pole has a smooth surface and is three-quarters of an inch in diameter.

After the poles were reduced to this state he whittled all the ends to the form of a truncated cone—that is, like a sharpened lead-pencil with the lead broken off (F, Fig. 70)—a blunt point. He next went to a tinsmith and had two sheet-iron cups made large enough to cover the eight pole-ends (G and G', Figs. 71 and 72). Each cup was six inches deep. After trying the cups, or thimbles, on the poles to see that they would fit, he made two moulds of oak. First he cut two pieces of oak plank two feet six

Fig. 77.—Umbrella canoe.

inches long by one foot six inches (H, Fig. 74), which he trimmed into the form shown by J, Fig. 75, making a notch to fit each of the round ribs, and to spread them as the ribs of an umbrella are spread. He made two other similar moulds for the bow and stern, each of which, of course, is smaller than the middle one. After spreading the ribs with the moulds, and bringing the ends together in the tin cups, he made holes in the bottom of the cups where the ends of the ribs came, and fastened the ribs to the cups with brass screws, fitted with leather washers, and run through the holes in the tin and screwed into the ends of the poles or ribs.

Fig. 78.—Canoe folded for transportation. Canoe in water in distance.

A square hole was then cut through each mould (K, Fig. 75), and the poles put in place, gathered together at the ends, and held in place by the tin thimbles. The square holes in the moulds allow several small, light floor planks to form a dry floor to the canoe.

The canvas costs about forty-five cents a yard, and five yards are all you need. The deck can be made of drilling, which comes about twenty-eight inches wide and costs about twenty cents a yard. Five yards of this will be plenty. Fit your canvas over the frame, stretch it tightly, and tack it securely to the two top ribs only. Fasten the deck on in the same manner.

When Mr. Dodge had the canoe covered and decked, with a square hole amidship to sit in, he put two good coats of paint on the canvas, allowed it to dry, and his boat was ready for use (Fig. 77). He quaintly says that "it looked like a starved dog, with all its ribs showing through the skin," just as the ribs of an umbrella show on top through the silk covering. But this does not in any way impede the progress of the boat through the water.

Where the moulds are the case is different, for the lines of the moulds cross the line of progress at right angles and must necessarily somewhat retard the boat.   But even this is not perceptible. The worst feature about the moulds is that the canvas is very apt to be damaged there by contact with the shore, float, or whatever object it rubs against.

With ordinary care the umbrella canoe

Will Last for Years

and is a good boat for paddling on inland streams and small bodies of water; and when you are through with it for the night, all that is necessary is to remove the stretchers by springing the poles from the notches in the spreaders, roll up the canvas around the poles, put it on your shoulder, and carry it home or to camp, as shown in Fig. 78.

To put your canoe together again put in the moulds, fit the poles in their places, and the umbrella is raised, or, rather, the canoe is, if we can use such an expression in regard to a boat.

CHAPTER VI

THE BIRCH-BARK

How to Build a Real Birch-Bark Canoe or a Canvas Canoe on a "Birch-Bark" Frame—How to Mend a Birch-Bark

ALTHOUGH the Indian was the first to build these simple little boats, some of his white brothers are quite as expert in the work. But the red man can outdo his white brother in navigating the craft. The only tools required in building a canoe are a knife and awl, a draw-shave and a hammer. An Indian can do all of his work with a knife.

Several years ago canvas began to be used extensively in canoe-building, instead of birch bark, and it will eventually entirely supersede birch, although nothing can be found that bends so gracefully. There are several canvas-canoe factories in Maine, and the canoes made of canvas have both the symmetry and the durability of the birches. They are also a trifle cheaper, but if the real thing and sentiment are wanted, one should never have anything but a bark craft.

If properly handled, a good canoe will safely hold four men. Canoes intended for deep water should have considerable depth. Those intended for shoal water, such as trout-fishers use, are made as flat as possible. Up to the time when canoeing was introduced the materials for building craft of this kind could be found all along the rivers. Big birch-trees grew in countless numbers, and clear, straight cedar was quite as plentiful within a few feet of the water's edge. Now one must go miles back into the dense forests for such materials, and even then seldom does it happen that two suitable trees are found within sight of one or the other. Cedar is more difficult of the two to find.

The Tree

The tree is selected, first, for straightness; second, smoothness; third, freedom from knots or limbs; fourth, toughness of bark; fifth, small size of eyes; sixth, length (the last is not so important, as two trees can be put together), and, seventh, size (which is also not so important, as the sides can be pieced out).

Dimensions

The average length of canoe is about 19 feet over all, running, generally, from 18 to 22 feet for a boat to be used on inland waters, the sea-going canoes being larger, with relatively higher bows. The average width is about 30 inches inside, measured along the middle cross-bar; the greatest width inside is several inches below the middle cross-bar, and is several inches greater than the width measured along said cross-bar.

The measurements given below are those of a canoe 19 feet over all: 16 feet long inside, measured along the curve of the gunwale; 30 inches wide inside. The actual length inside is less than 16 feet, but the measurement along the gunwales is the most important.

Bark

Bark can be peeled when the sap is flowing or when the tree is not frozen—at any time in late spring, summer, and early fall (called summer bark); in winter during a thaw, when the tree is not frozen, and when the sap may have begun to flow.

Difference in the Bark

Summer bark peels readily, is smooth inside, of a yellow color, which turns reddish upon exposure to the sun, and is chalky-gray in very old canoes. Winter bark adheres closely, and forcibly brings up part of the inner bark, which on exposure turns dark red. This rough surface may be moistened and scraped away. All winter-bark canoes must be thus scraped and made smooth. Sometimes the dark red is left in the form of a decorative pattern extending around the upper edge of the canoe, the rest of the surface being scraped smooth.

Process of Peeling

The tree should be cut down so that the bark can be removed more easily.

A log called a skid (Fig. 79) is laid on the ground a few feet from the base of the tree, which will keep the butt of the tree off the ground when the tree is felled.   The limbs at the top will

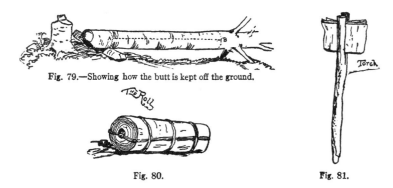

Fig. 79.—Showing how the butt is kept off the ground.

Fig. 80.

Fig. 81.

keep the other end off the ground.   A space is cleared of bushes and obstructions where the tree is to fall.

After the tree has been cut down, a cut is made in a straight line (A, B, Fig. 79), splitting the bark from top to bottom, and a ring cut at A and B (Fig. 79).   When sap is flowing, the bark is readily removed; but in winter the edges of the cut are raised with a knife, and a thin, pliant hard-wood knife or "spud" is pushed around under the bark.

Toasting

After the bark has dropped upon the ground the inside surface is warmed with a torch, which softens and straightens it out flat. The torch is made of a bundle of birch bark held in a split stick (Fig. 81).

It is then rolled up like a carpet, with inside surface out, and tightly bound, generally with cedar bark when the latter can be procured (Fig. 80).

If the tree is long enough, a piece is taken off at least nineteen feet in length, so that the ends of the canoe may not be pieced out. A few shorter pieces are wrapped up with the bundle for piecing out the sides.

The Roll

is taken on the back in an upright position, and is carried by a broad band of cedar bark, passing under the lower end of the roll and around in front of the breast and shoulders (Fig. 82).

Fig. 82.—Mode of carrying roll.

Effects of Heat

It is laid where the sun will not shine on it and harden it. The first effect of heat is to make it pliant. Long exposure to heat or to dry atmosphere makes it hard and brittle.

The Woodwork

is as follows:

Five cross-bars of rock-maple (Figs. 83, 85, and 91). All the rest is of white cedar, taken from the heart. The sap-wood absorbs water, and would make the canoe too heavy, so it is rejected. The wood requires to be straight and clear, and it is best to use perfectly green wood for the ribs.

Two strips 16½ feet long, 1½ inch square, tapering toward either end, the ends being notched (Fig. 83 A) is a section of the 16½ foot strip.   Each strip is mortised for the cross-bars (see Fig. 85). The lower outside edge is bevelled off to receive the ends of the ribs.

The dimensions of the cross-bars (Fig. 85) are 12 x 2 x ½ inch, 22½ x 2 x ¾ inch, and 30 x 2 x ⅞ inch.   The cross-bars are placed in position, and the ends of the gunwales are tied with spruce

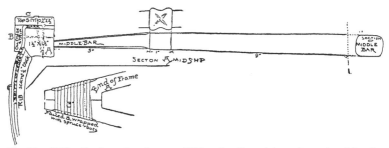

Figs. 83 and 83½.—Showing section of canoe amidship and section and shape of gunwale and top view.

roots after being nailed together to prevent splitting.   Each bar is held in place by a peg of hard wood.

For stitching and wrapping, long, slender roots of spruce, or sometimes of elm, are peeled and split in two.   Black ash splits are rarely used except for repairing (Figs. 86, 87, 88).

Next we need (B, Fig. 83) two strips 1 or 1¼ inch by ½ inch, a little over 19 feet long, to go outside of gunwales, and (C, Fig. 83) two top strips, same length, 2 inches wide in middle, tapering to 1 inch at either end, 1½ inch thick.

Ribs

About fifty in number (Figs. 91, 92) are split with the grain (F, Fig. 92), so that the heart side of the wood will be on the inner side when the rib is bent.   The wood bends better this way. They must be perfectly straight-grained and free from knots.

Ribs for the middle are four inches wide, ribs for the ends about three inches wide (Fig. 91 and G, Fig. 92), and are whittled down to a scant half an inch (Fig. 93). Green wood is generally used, and before it has had any time to season. The ribs may be soft-

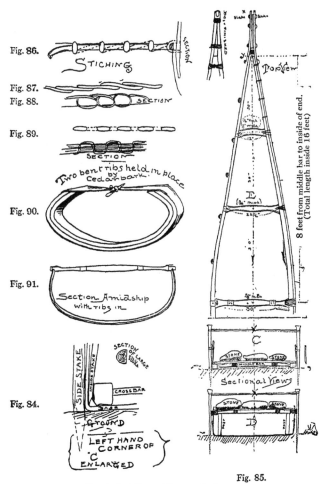

Fig. 86.

Fig. 87.

Fig. 88.

Fig. 89.

Fig. 90.

Fig. 91.

Fig. 84.

Fig. 85.

Details of sticking and framework of canoe.

ened by pouring hot water on them, and should be bent in pairs to prevent breaking (Fig. 90). They are held in shape by a band of cedar bark passed around outside.

The ribs are of importance in the shaping of the canoe. The sides bulge out (Figs. 91, 92). The shape of the ribs determines the depth and stability of the canoe.

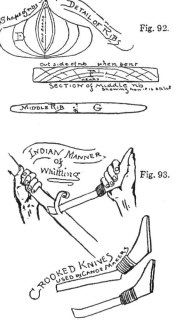

Fig. 92.

Fig. 93.

Details of ribs, Indian knives and method of using them.

Lining Strips

Other strips, an eighth of an inch thick, are carefully whittled out, with straight edges. They are a little over eight feet long, and are designed to be laid inside on the bark, edge to edge, between the bark and the ribs. These strips lap an inch or two where they meet, in the middle of the canoe, and are wider here than at the ends, owing to the greater circumference of the canoe in the middle.

Seasoning

All the timber is carefully tied up before building and laid away. The ribs are allowed to season perfectly, so that they will keep their shape and not spring back.

The Bed

Next the bed is prepared on a level spot, if possible shaded from the sun. A space is levelled about three and a half feet wide and a little longer than the canoe. The surface is made perfectly smooth. The middle is one or two inches higher than either end.

Building

The frame is laid exactly in the middle of the bed. A small post is driven in the ground (Fig. 94), on which each end of the frame will rest. Stakes, two or three feet long and about two

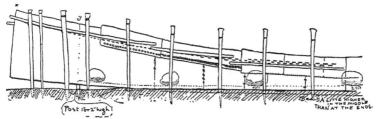

Fig. 94.—Showing stakes supporting bark sides; note stones on the bottom.

inches in diameter, are whittled flat on one side, and are driven with the flat side toward the frame at the following points, leaving a space of about a quarter of an inch between the stake and the frame (Fig. 94): One stake an inch or two on either side of each cross-bar, and another stake half way between each cross-bar. This makes eleven stakes on each side of the frame. Twelve additional stakes are driven as follows: One pair facing each other, at the end of the frame; another pair, an inch apart, about six inches from the last pair, measuring toward the ends of the canoe; and another pair, an inch apart, a foot from these. These last stakes will be nine and a half feet from the middle of the frame, and nineteen feet from the corresponding stakes at the other end. Next, these stakes are all taken up, and the frame laid aside.

To Soften the Bark

Next the bark is unrolled. If it has laid until it has become a little hardened, it is placed in the river or stream for a day or two. It is spread out flat, and laid upon the bed with the gray or outside surface up. The inside surface is placed downward, and becomes the outside of the canoe.

The frame is replaced upon the bark, so that it will be at the same distance from each side and end of the bed that it was before. At each cross-bar boards are laid across the frame, and heavy stones are laid upon them to keep the frame solid and immovable upon the bark (Fig. 85, C). The edges of the bark are next bent up in a perpendicular position, and in order that it may bend smoothly slits are made in the bark in an outward direction, at right angles to the frame. A cut is made close to the end of each cross-bar, and one half way between each bar, which is generally sufficient to allow the bark to be bent up smoothly. As the bark is bent up, the large stakes are slipped back in the holes which they occupied before, and the tops of each opposite pair are connected with a strip of cedar bark which keeps the stakes perfectly perpendicular. At each end it is necessary to take out a small triangular piece or gore, so that the edges may come together without overlapping.

Next twenty-two pieces of cedar, one to two feet long, and about $\frac{1}{2}$ or $\frac{3}{4}$ inch thick, are split out, and whittled thin and flat at one end. This sharpened edge is inserted between the outside edge of the frame and the bent-up bark, opposite each large stake. The other end of the chisel-shaped piece is tightly tied to the large stake outside. By means of the *large outside stake* and the inside "*stake*," so-called, the bark is held in a perfectly upright position; and in order to keep the bent-up part more perfectly flat and smooth, the strips of cedar are pushed in lengthwise between the stakes and the bark, on each side of the bark, as shown in sectional views (Fig. 85, C, D).

Sometimes, in place of having temporary strips to go on outside of the bark, the long outside strip (B, Fig. 83), is slipped in place instead.

It may now be seen if the bark is not wide enough. If it is not, the sides must be pieced out with a narrow piece, cut in such a way that the eyes in the bark will run in the same direction as those of the large piece.

As a general rule, from the middle to the next bar the strip for piecing is placed on the inside of the large piece, whose upper edge has previously been trimmed straight, and the two are sewed together by the stitch shown in Fig. 86, the spruce root being passed over another root laid along the trimmed-off edge of the large piece of bark to prevent the stitches from tearing out. From the second bar to the end of the canoe, or as far as may be necessary, the strip is placed outside the large piece, and from the second to the end bar is sewed as in Fig. 87, and from the end bar to the end of the canoe is stitched as in Fig. 88.

Next, the weights are taken off the frame, which is raised up as follows, the bark remaining flat on the bed as before:

A post eight inches long is set up under each end of middle cross-bar (Fig. 85, D), one end resting on the bark and the other end supporting either end of the middle cross-bar. Another post, nine inches long, is similarly placed under each end of the next cross-bar. Another, twelve inches long, is placed under each end of the end cross-bar; and another, sixteen and a half or seventeen inches, supports each end of the frame.

As the posts are placed under each cross-bar, the weights are replaced; and as these posts are higher at the ends than in the middle, the proper curve is obtained for the gunwales. The temporary strips, that have been placed outside the bent-up portion of the bark, are removed, and the long outside strip before mentioned (B, Fig. 83) is slipped in place between the outside stakes and the bark. This strip is next nailed to the frame with wrought-iron nails that pass through the bark and are clinched on the inside. This outside strip has taken exactly the curve of the frame, but its upper edge, before nailing, was raised so as to be out an eighth of an inch (or the thickness of the bark) higher than the top surface of the frame, so that when the edges of the bark have been bent down, and tacked flat to the frame, a level surface will be presented, upon which the wide top strip will eventually be nailed.   Formerly the outer strip was bound to the frame with roots every few inches, but now it is nailed.

The cross-bars are now lashed to the frame, having previously been held only by a peg.   The roots are passed through holes in the end of the bars, around the outside strip (see right-hand side of Fig. 85).   A two-inch piece of the bark, which has been tacked

Fig. 95.—Shows how to describe arc of circle for bow, also ornamentation of winter bark.

down upon the frame, is removed at the ends by the cross-bars, where the spruce roots are to pass around, and the outside strip is cut away to a corresponding extent, so that the roots, when wrapped around, will be flush with the surface above.

All the stakes are now removed, and laid away to be ready for the next canoe that may be built, and the canoe taken upside down upon two horses or benches, that will keep the craft clear of the ground.

The shape of the bow is now marked out, either by the eye or with mechanical aid, according to the following rule: An arc of a circle, with a radius of seventeen inches, is described (Fig. 95) having as a centre a point shown in diagram.   The bark is then cut away to this line.

Bow-piece

To stiffen the bow, a bow-piece of cedar, nearly three feet long (Fig. 96), an inch and a half wide, and half an inch thick on one edge, bevelled and rounded off toward the other edge, is needed. To facilitate bending edgeways it is split into four or five sections (as in Fig. 98) for about thirty inches.   The end that remains unsplit is notched on its thicker edge (Fig. 96) to receive the lower end of an oval cedar board (Fig. 97) that is placed upright in the bow underneath the tip of the frame. It is bent to correspond with the curve of the boat, with the thin edge toward the outside of the circle, and wrapped with twine, so that it will keep its shape. The bow-piece is placed between the edges of the bark, which are then sewed together by an over-and-over stitch, which passes through the bow-piece.

A pitch is prepared of rosin and grease, in such proportions that it will neither readily crack in cold water nor melt in the sun. One or the other ingredient is added until by test it is found just right.

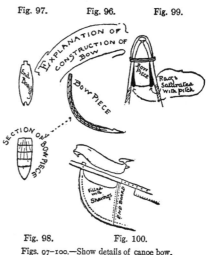

Fig. 97.   Fig. 96.   Fig. 99.

Fig. 98.   Fig. 100.

Figs. 97–100.—Show details of canoe bow.

Patching and Pitching

The canoe is now placed on the ground, right side up, and all holes are covered on the inside with thin birch bark that is pasted down with hot pitch. A strip of cloth is saturated with hot pitch, and pressed into the cracks on either side of the bow-piece inside, between the bark and the bow-piece (Fig. 99).

The thin longitudinal strips are next laid in position, edge to edge, lapping several inches by the middle; they are whittled thin here so as to lap evenly.

The ribs are next tightly driven in place, commencing at the small end ones and working toward the middle. The end ribs may be two or three inches apart, being closer toward the middle, where, in many cases, they touch. Usually, they are about half an inch apart in the middle. Each rib is driven into place with a square-ended stick and a mallet.

The ends are stuffed with shavings (Fig. 100 and "Section" Fig. 100½), and an oval cedar board is put in the place formerly occupied by the post that supported the end of the frame. The lower end rests in the notch of the bow-piece, while the upper is cut with two shoulders that fit underneath each side of the frame; Fig. 97 shows the cedar board.

The top strip is next nailed on to the frame. Almost always a piece of bark, a foot or more long, and nine or ten inches wide, is bent and slipped under, between both top and side strips and the bark. The ends of this piece hang down about three inches below the side strips. The loose ends of the strips are bound together, as in diagram, and the projecting tips of both strips and bow-piece are trimmed off close.

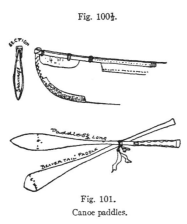

Fig. 100½.

Fig. 101.
Canoe paddles.

Next the canoe is turned upside down. If winter bark has been used, the surface is moistened and the roughness scraped off with a knife. Generally the red rough surface is left in the form of a decorative pattern several inches wide around the upper edge (Fig. 95). Sometimes the maker's name and date are left in this way.

Finally, a strip of stout canvas, three or four inches wide, is dipped in the melted pitch and laid on the stitching at the ends, extending up sufficiently far above the water-line. All cracks and seams are covered with pitch, laid on with a small wooden paddle. While still soft, a wet finger or the palm of the hand is rubbed over the pitch to smooth it down before it hardens.

Leaks

Water is placed inside, and the leaky places marked, to be stopped when dry. A can of rosin is usually carried in the canoe, and when a leak occurs, the canoe is taken out of the water, the

Fig. 101½.—From photograph of Indian building a birch-bark canoe.

leak discovered by sucking, the place dried with a torch of wood or birch bark, and the pitch applied.

Paddles are made of rock maple, and sometimes of birch and even cedar. Bow paddles are usually longer and narrower in the blade than stern paddles (Fig. 101).

Bottom Protection

Sometimes the canoe is shod with "shoes," or strips of cedar, laid lengthwise and tied to the outside of the bark with ash splits that pass through holes in the cedar shoes, and are brought up around the sides of the canoe and tied to each cross-bar. This protects the bottom of the boat from the sharp rocks that abound in some rapid streams.

All canoes are of the general shape of the one described, though this is considerably varied in different localities, some being built with high rolling bows, some slender, some wider, some nearly straight on the bottom, others decidedly curved.

Besides the two paddles the canoe should carry a pole ten feet long, made of a slender spruce, whittled so as to be about one and three-fourths inch in diameter in the middle and smaller at either end, and having at one end either a ring and a spike or else a pointed cap of iron.   The pole is used for propelling the canoe up swift streams.   This, says Tappan Adney, "is absolutely indispensable."   The person using the pole stands in one end, or nearer the middle if alone, and pushes the canoe along close to the bank, so as to take advantage of the eddies, guiding the canoe with one motion, only to be learned by practice, and keeping the pole usually on the side next the bank.   Where the streams have rocky and pebbly bottoms poling is easy, but in muddy or soft bottoms it is tiresome work; muddy bottoms, however, are not usually found in rapid waters.

A Canvas Canoe

can be made by substituting canvas in the place of birch bark; and if it is kept well painted it makes not only a durable but a very beautiful boat.   The writer once owned a canvas canoe that was at least fifteen years old and still in good condition.

About six yards of ten-ounce cotton canvas, fifty inches wide, will be sufficient to cover a canoe, and it will require two papers of four-ounce copper tacks to secure the canvas on the frame.

The boat should be placed, deck down, upon two "horses" or wooden supports, such as you see carpenters and builders use.

Fold the canvas lengthwise, so as to find the centre, then tack the centre of one end of the cloth to top of bow-piece, or stem, using two or three tacks to hold it securely.   Stretch the cloth the length of the boat, pull it taut, with the centre line of the canvas over the keel line of the canoe, and tack the centre of the other end of the cloth to the top of the stern-piece.

If care has been taken thus far, an equal portion of the covering will lap the gunwale on each side of the boat.

Begin amidships and drive the tacks, about two inches apart, along the gunwale and an inch below the deck (on the outside). Tack about two feet on one side, pull the cloth tightly across, and tack it about three feet on the other side. Continue to alternate, tacking on one side and then the other, until finished.

With the hands and fingers knead the cloth so as to thicken or "full" it where it would otherwise wrinkle, and it will be possible to stretch the canvas without cutting it over the frame.

The cloth that projects beyond the gunwale may be used for the deck, or it may be cut off after bringing it over and tacking upon the inside of the gunwale, leaving the canoe open like a birch-bark.

To Paddle a Canoe

No one can expect to learn to paddle a canoe from a book, however explicit the directions may be. There is only one way to learn to swim and that is by going into the water and trying it, and the only proper way to learn to paddle a canoe is to paddle one until you catch the knack.

In the ordinary canoe, to be found at the summer watering places, there are cane seats and they are always too high for safety. A top load on any sort of a boat is always dangerous, and every real canoeist seats his passengers on the bottom of the boat and kneels on the bottom himself while paddling. Of course, one's knees will feel more comfortable if there is some sort of a cushion under them, and a passenger will be less liable to get wet if he has a pneumatic cushion on which to sit. No expert canoeist paddles alternately first on the one side, and then on the other; on the contrary, he takes pride in his ability to keep his paddle continuously on either side that suits his convenience.

The Indians of the North Woods are probably the best paddlers, and from them we can take points in the art. It is from them we first learned the use of the canoe, for our open canvas canoes of to-day are practically modelled on the lines of the old birch-barks.

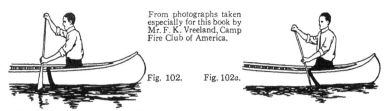

From photographs taken
especially for this book by
Mr. F. K. Vreeland, Camp
Fire Club of America.

Fig. 102.　　Fig. 102a.

Fig. 102.—Beginning of stroke. Paddle should not be reached farther forward than this. It is immersed *edgewise* (not point first) with a slicing motion. Note the angle of paddle—rear face of blade turned *outward* to avoid tendency of canoe to turn. Staff of paddle is 6 inches too short. Left hand should be lower.

Fig. 102a.—A moment later. Right hand pushing forward, left hand swinging down. Left hand should be lower on full-sized paddle.

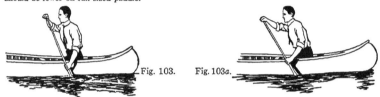

Fig. 103.　　Fig. 103a.

Fig. 103.—Putting the power of the body in the stroke by bending slightly forward. Left hand held stationary from now on, to act as fulcrum. The power comes from the right arm and shoulders.

Fig. 103a.—The final effort, full weight of the body on the paddle. The right arm and body are doing the work, the left arm (which is weak at this point) acting as fulcrum. Note twist of the right wrist to give blade the proper angle.

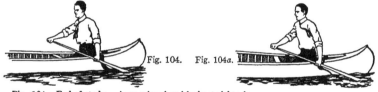

Fig. 104.　　Fig. 104a.

Fig. 104.—End of stroke. Arms relaxed and body straightening.

Fig. 104a.—Beginning of recovery. Paddle slides out of water gently. Note that blade is perfectly flat on the surface. No steering action is required. If the canoe tends to swerve it is because the *stroke* was not correct. Only a duffer *steers* with his paddle after the stroke is over. The left hand now moves forward, the right swinging out and back, moving paddle forward horizontally.

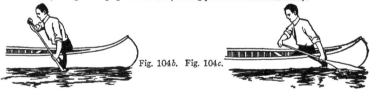

Fig. 104b.　　Fig. 104c.

Fig. 104b—Turning to right. The latter part of a broad sweep outward, away from the canoe. The blade is now being swept toward the canoe, the left hand pulling in, the right pushing out. Position of right wrist shows that blade has the opposite slant to that shown in the straightaway stroke—*i. e.*, the near face of blade is turned *inward*. Blade leaves water with *outer* edge up. Wake of canoe shows sharpness of turn.

Fig. 104c.—Turning to left. The last motion of a stroke in which the paddle is swept close to the canoe with the blade turned much farther outward than in the straightaway stroke. At end of stroke blade is given an outward sweep, and leaves the water with the *inner* edge up. *This is not a steering* or dragging motion. It is a powerful sweep of the paddle. Note swirl in wake of canoe showing sharp turn.

64

When you are standing upright and your paddle is in front of you with the blade upon the ground, the handle should reach to your eye-brows. (See Figs. 101, 102, 103, etc.)

Kneel with the paddle across the canoe and not farther forward than the knees. Then dip the blade *edgewise* (not point first) by raising the upper hand without bending the elbow. Swing the paddle back, keeping it close to the canoe, and give a little twist to the upper wrist to set the paddle at the proper angle shown in the photos. The exact angle depends upon the trim of the boat, the wind, etc., and must be such that the canoe does not swerve *at any part* of the stroke, but travels straight ahead. The lower arm acts mainly as a fulcrum and does not move back and forth more than a foot. The power comes from the upper arm and shoulder, and the body bends forward as the weight is thrown on the paddle. The stroke continues until the paddle slides out of the water endwise, flat on the surface. Then for recovery the blade is brought forward by a swing from the shoulder, *not* lifting it vertically, but swinging it horizontally with the blade parallel to the water and the upper hand low. When it reaches a point opposite the knee it is slid into the water again, edgewise, for another stroke. The motion is a more or less rotary one, like stirring cake, not a simple movement back and forth.

To Carry a Canoe

To pick up a canoe and carry it requires not only the knack but also muscle, and no undeveloped boy should make the attempt, as he might strain himself, with serious results. But there are plenty of young men—good, husky fellows—who can learn to do this without any danger of injury if they are taught *how* to lift by a competent physical instructor.

To pick up a canoe for a "carry," stoop over and grasp the middle brace with the right arm extended, and a short hold with the left hand, as shown in Fig. 105.

When you have a secure hold, hoist the canoe up on your legs, as shown in Fig. 106. Without stopping the motion give her another boost, until you have the canoe with the upper side above your head, as in Fig. 107. In the diagram the paddles are not

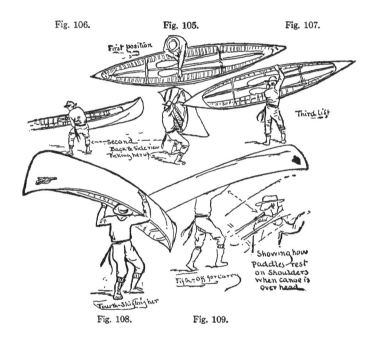

Fig. 106.   Fig. 105.   Fig. 107.

First position

Third Lift

Second
Back & Side view
Picking her up

Showing how
Paddles rest
on Shoulders
when canoe is
over head.

Fifth-Off for Carry

Fourth-Sliding her

Fig. 108.   Fig. 109.

spread apart as far as they should be. If the paddles are too close together a fall may break ones neck.

Now turn the canoe over your head and slide your head between the paddles (which are lashed to the spreaders, as shown in Fig. 105), and twist your body around as you let the canoe settle down over your head (Fig. 108). If you have a sweater or a coat, it will help your shoulders by making a roll of it to serve as a pad under the paddles, as in Fig. 109. I have seen an Indian carry a canoe in this manner on a dog-trot over a five-mile portage without resting. I also have seen Indians carry canoes over mountains, crossing by the celebrated Ladder Portage in western

THE FIRST TO CROSS
THE LADDER PORTAGE

Fig. 110.—Northern Quebec Indians crossing the "ladder portage."

Quebec, where the only means of scaling a cliff is by ascending a ladder made of notched logs. For real canoe work it is necessary that a man should know how to carry his craft across country from one body of water to another. All through the Lakelands of Canada, and also the Lake St. John district, up to Hudson Bay itself, the only trails are by water, with portage across from one stream or lake to the other.

CHAPTER VII

HOW TO BUILD A PADDLING DORY

A Simple Boat Which Any One Can Build—The Cheapest Sort of a Boat

To construct this craft it is, of course, necessary that we shall have some lumber, but we will use the smallest amount and the expense will come within the limits of a small purse.

First we must have two boards, their lengths depending upon circumstances and the lumber available. The ones in the diagram are supposed to be of pine to measure (after being trimmed) 18 feet long by 18 inches wide and about 1 inch thick. When the boards are trimmed down so as to be exact duplicates of each other, place one board over the other so that their edges all fit exactly and then nail each end of the two boards together for the distance of about six inches. Turn the boards over and nail them upon the opposite side in the same manner, clamping the nail ends if they protrude. Do this by holding the head of a hammer or a stone against the heads of the nails while you hold a wire nail against the protruding end, and with a hammer bend it over the nail until it can be mashed flat against the board so that it will not project beyond its surface.

After you have proceeded thus far, take some pieces of tin (Fig. 112) and bend the ragged edges over, so as to make a clean, straight fold, and hammer it down flat until there are no rough or raw edges exposed. Now tack a piece of this tin over the end of the boards which composed the sides of the boat, as in Fig. 114. Make the holes for the tacks first by driving the pointed end of a wire nail through the tin where you wish the tacks to go and then tack the tin snugly and neatly on, after which tack on another piece of tin on both bow and stern, as in Fig. 116. This will hold the two ends of the boards securely together so that they may be carefully sprung apart in the middle to receive the middle mould which is to hold them in shape until the bottom of the boat is nailed on, and the permanent thwarts, or seats, fastened inside. When the latter are permanently fixed they will keep the boat in shape.

To make the mould, which is only a temporary thing, you may use any rough board, or boards nailed together with cleats

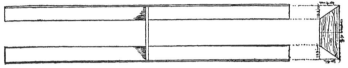

Fig. 111.—Parts of dory.

to hold them. The mould should be 2 feet 6 inches long and 1 foot 4 inches high. Fig. 111 will show you how to cut off the ends to give the proper slant. The dotted lines show the board before it is trimmed in shape. By measuring along the edge of the board from each end 10.8 inches and marking the points, and then, with a carpenter's pencil ruling the diagonal lines to the other edge and ends of the board, the triangles may be sawed off with a hand saw.

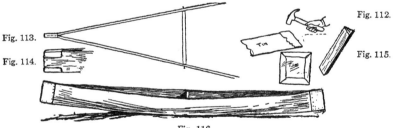

Fig. 112.

Fig. 113.

Fig. 114.

Fig. 115.

Fig. 116.
The simple details of the dory.

Fig. 111 shows where the mould is to be placed in the center of the two side boards. As the boards in this diagram are supposed to be on the slant, and consequently in the perspective, they do not appear as wide as they really are. The diagram is made also with the ends of the side boards free so as to better show the position of the mould. But when the side boards are sprung apart and the mould placed in position (Fig. 113), it will appear as in Fig. 116 or Fig. 117. Fig. 115 shows the shape of the stem-posts to be set in both bow and stern and nailed securely in place.

When you have gone thus far fit in two temporary braces near the bow and stern, as shown in Fig. 117. These braces are sim-

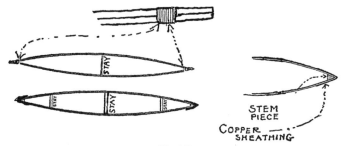

Fig. 118.
Top views of dory and parts of dory.

ply narrow pieces of boards held in position by nails driven through the outside of the boat, the latter left with their heads protruding, sc that they may be easily drawn when necessary.

Now turn the boat over bottom up and you will find that the angle at which the sides are bent will cause the bottom boards to rest upon a thin edge of the side boards, as shown in Fig. 119. With an ordinary jack-plane trim this down so that the bottom boards will rest flush and snug, as in Fig. 120.

How to Calk a Boat so That It Won't Leak

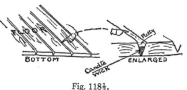

Fig. 118½.

If you wish to make a bottom that will never leak, not even when it is placed in the water for the first time, plane off the boards on their sides, so that when fitted together they will leave a triangular groove between each board; as shown in Fig. 118½. These grooves will show upon the inside of the boat, and not upon the outside, and in this case the calking is done from the inside and not from the outside. They are first calked with candlewick, over which putty is used, but for a rough boat it is not even necessary to use any calking. When the planks swell they will be forced together, so as to exclude all water.

To fasten the bottom on the boat put a board lengthwise at the end, as shown in Fig. 121. One end shows the end board as it is first nailed on, and the other end shows it after it has been trimmed off to correspond with the sides of the boat. Now put your short pieces of boards for the bottom on one at a time, driving each one snug up against its neighbor before nailing it in place and leaving

Fig. 117.

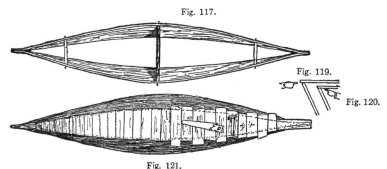

Fig. 119.

Fig. 120.

Fig. 121.
Top view with sides in place, also reversed view showing how bottom boards are laid.

the rough or irregular ends of each board protrude on each side, as shown at the right-hand end of Fig. 121.

When all the boards are nailed in place (by beginning at one end and fitting them against each other until the other end is reached) they may be trimmed off with a saw (Fig. 121) and your boat is finished with the exception of the thwarts, or seats.

If you intend to propel this with paddles like a canoe, you will need a seat in the centre for your passenger, and this may be placed in the position occupied by the form (Figs. 111 and 117) after the latter is removed. To fit a seat in it is only necessary to cut two cleats and nail them to the sides of the boat for the seat to rest upon and saw off a board the proper length to fit upon the cleats. It would be well now to fasten the braces in the bow and stern permanently, adjusting them to suit your convenience. The seat should be as low as possible for safety. With this your paddling dory is finished, and may be used even without being painted. A coat of paint, however, improves not only the looks but the tightness and durability of any boat.

We have now advanced so far in our boat-building that it becomes necessary that the beginner should learn more about boats and boating, and since this book is written for beginners, we will take it for granted that they know absolutely nothing about the subject and will give all the rudimentary knowledge for landlubbers in the next chapter.

CHAPTER VIII

THE LANDLUBBER'S CHAPTER

Common Nautical Terms and Expressions Defined—How to Sail a Boat—Boat Rigs—Rowing-clothes—How to Make a Bathing-suit—How to Avoid Sunburn

THERE are a few common terms with which all who venture on the water should be familiar, not only for convenience, but for prudential reasons.

Accidents are liable to happen to boats of all descriptions, and often the safety of property and life depend upon the passengers' ability to understand what is said to them by the officers or sailors in charge of the craft.

To those who are familiar with the water and shipping it may seem absurd to define the bow and stern of a boat, but there are people who will read this book who cannot tell the bow from the stern, so we will begin this chapter with the statement that

The bow is the front end of the boat, and

The stern is the rear end of the boat.

For'ard is toward the bow of the boat.

Aft is toward the stern of the boat. Both terms are used by sailors as forward and backward are used by landsmen.

The hull is the boat itself without masts, spars, or rigging. A skiff and a birch-bark canoe are hulls.

The keel is the piece of timber running along the centre of the bottom of the hull, like the runner of a skate, and used to give the boat a hold on the water, so that she will not slide sideways.

When you are sitting in the stern of a boat, facing the bow, the side next to your right hand is the right-hand side of the boat, and the side next to your left hand is the left-hand side of the boat. But these terms are not used by seamen; they always say **Starboard** for the right-hand side of the boat, and **Port** for the left-hand side of the boat. Formerly the left-hand side was called the larboard, but this occasioned many serious

Port.

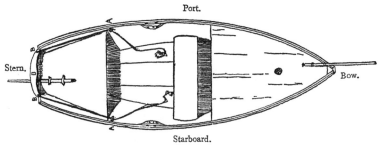

Stern.

Bow.

Starboard.

Fig. 122.—Top view of small boat.

mistakes on account of the similarity of the sound of larboard and starboard when used in giving orders.

Red and Green Lights

After dark a red light is carried on the port side and a green light on the starboard side of all vessels in motion. If you can remember that port wine is red, and that the port light is of the same color, you will always be able to tell in which direction an approaching craft is pointing by the relative location of the lights.

> "When both lights you see ahead,
> Port your helm and show your red!
> Green to green and red to red,
> You're all right, and go ahead!"

If you are a real landlubber, the verse quoted will be of little service, because you will not know how to port your helm. In fact, you probably will not know where to look for the helm or what it looks like; but only a few of our readers are out-and-out landlubbers, and most of them know that the helm is in some way connected with the steering apparatus.

The rudder is the movable piece of board at the stern of the boat by means of which the craft is guided. The rudder is moved by a lever, ropes, or a wheel.

The tiller is the lever for moving the rudder, or the ropes used for the same purpose (Fig. 123).

Fig. 123.—Helm—Lever, or stick, for tiller.

The wheel is the wheel whose spokes end in handles on the outer edge of the rim, or felly, and it is used for moving the rudder (Fig. 124).

The helm is that particular part of the steering apparatus that you put your hands on when steering.

The deck is the roof of the hull.

The centreboard is an adjustable keel that can be raised or lowered at pleasure. It is an American invention. The centreboard, as a rule, is only used on comparatively small vessels. The inventor of the centreboard is Mr. Salem Wines, who kept a shop on Water Street, near Market Slip, and, when alive, was a well-known New York boat-builder. His body now lies in Greenwood Cemetery, and upon the headstone of his grave is the inscription, "The Inventor of the Centreboard."

For sailing, the boat, or hull, is rigged with masts and spars for spreading the sails to catch the wind.

The masts are the upright poles, or sticks, that hold the sails.

Fig. 124.—Helm—The wheel.

The yards are the poles, or sticks, at right angles with the masts that spread the sails.

The boom is the movable spar at the bottom of the sail.

The gaff is the pole, or spar, for spreading the top, or head, of the sail (Fig. 125).

The sail is a big canvas kite, of which the boom, gaff, and masts are the kite-sticks. You must not understand by this that the sail goes soaring up in the air, for the weight of the hull prevents that; but if you make fast a large kite to the mast of a boat it would be a sail, and if you had a line long and strong enough, and should fasten any spread sail to it, there can be no doubt that the sail would fly.

The **spars** are the masts, bowsprit, yards, and gaffs.

The **bowsprit** is the stick, or sprit, projecting from the bow of the boat (Fig. 161, Sloop).

The **foremast** is the mast next to the bow—the forward mast (Fig. 159, Ship).

The **mainmast** is the second mast—the mast next to the foremast.

Mizzen-mast is the mast next to and back of the mainmast (Fig. 159, Ship).

The **rigging** of a boat consists of the ropes, or lines, attached to its masts and sails, but a boat's rig refers to the number of masts as well as to the shape of its sails.

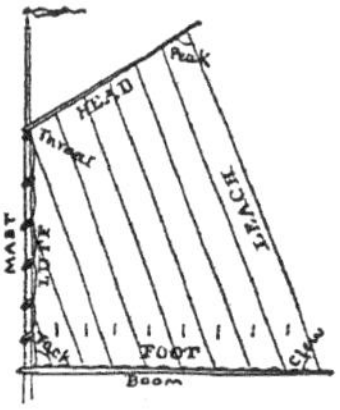

Fig. 125.—A sail.

Stays are strong ropes supporting the masts, fore and aft.

Shrouds are strong ropes reaching from the mastheads to the sides of the vessel; supports for the masts, starboard and port.

Ratlines are the little ropes that form the steps, or foot ropes, that run crosswise between the shrouds.

The **painter** is the rope at the bow of a small boat, used for the same purpose as is a hitching-strap on a horse.

The **standing rigging** consists of the stays and shrouds.

The **running rigging** consists of all the ropes used in handling yards and sails.

The **sheets** are the ropes, or lines, attached to the corners of sails, by which they are governed (Fig. 126).

The **main sheet** is the rope that governs the mainsail.

The **jib-sheet** is the rope that governs the jib-sail.

The **gaskets** are the ropes used in lashing the sails when furled.

The **braces** are the ropes used in swinging the yards around.

The **jib-stay** is the stay that runs from the foremast to the bowsprit.

The **bob-stay** is practically an extension of the jib-stay and the chief support of the spars. It connects the bow of the boat with the bowsprit and prevents the latter from bobbing up and down.

Besides the port and starboard sides of a boat there are the windward and leeward sides. Do not understand by this that the boat has four sides, like a square. Windward may be the port or the starboard side, according to the direction the wind blows; because

Windward means the side of the boat against which the wind blows—the side where the wind climbs aboard; or it may mean the direction from which the wind comes. The opposite side is called

Leeward—that is, the side of the boat opposite to that against which the wind blows, where the wind tumbles overboard, or the side opposite to windward. When you are sailing you may be near a

Lee Shore—that is, the shore on your lee side against which the wind blows; or a

Windward Shore—that is, the land on your windward side from which the wind blows.

All seamen dread a lee shore, as it is a most dangerous shore to approach, from the fact that the wind is doing its best to blow you on the rocks or beach. But the windward shore can be approached with safety, because the wind will keep you off the rocks, and if it is blowing hard, the land will break the force of the wind.

In a canoe or shell the boatman sits either directly on the bottom, or, as in the shell, very close to it, and the weight of his body serves to keep the boat steady, but larger crafts seldom rely upon live weights to steady them. They use

Ballast—that is, weights of stone, lead, iron, or sand-bags, used to balance the boat and make her steady.

As has been said before in this chapter, the sail is a big canvas kite made fast to the boat and called a sail, but the ordinary kite has its covering stretched permanently on rigid sticks.

The sail, however, can be stretched to its full extent or only partially, or it may be rolled up, exposing nothing but the masts to the force of the wind.　To accomplish all this there are various ropes and attachments, all of which are named.

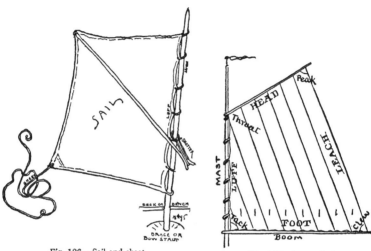

Fig. 126.—Sail and sheet.

Fig. 127.—Parts of sail.

It is quite important that the beginner should know the names of all the

Parts of a Sail

Luff.—That part of the sail adjoining the mast—the front of the sail (Fig. 127).

Leach.—That part of the sail stretched between the outer or after end of the boom and the outer end of the gaff—the back part of the sail (Fig. 127).

Head.—That part of the sail adjoining the gaff—the top of the sail.

Foot.—That part of the sail adjoining the boom—the bottom of the sail (Fig. 127).

Clews.—A general name for the four corners of the sail.

Clew.—The particular corner at the foot of the sail where the leach and boom meet (Fig. 127).

Tack.—The corner of the sail where boom and mast meet (Fig. 127).

Throat, or Nock.—The corner of the sail where gaff and mast meet (Fig. 127).

Peak.—Corner of the sail where the leach and gaff meet (Fig. 127).

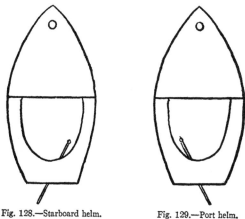

Fig. 128.—Starboard helm.   Fig. 129.—Port helm.

How to Steer a Boat

When you wish your boat to turn to the right push your helm to the left. This will push the rudder to the right and turn the boat in that direction. When you wish your boat to turn to the left push your helm to the right. In other words, starboard your helm and you will turn to the port (Fig. 128). Port your helm and you will turn to the starboard (Fig. 129).

From a reference to the diagram you may see that when you **port your helm** you move the tiller to the port side of the boat, and when you **starboard your helm** you move your tiller to the starboard side of the boat (Fig. 128), but to **ease your helm** you move your helm toward the centre of the boat—that is, amidships.

How to Sail a Boat

If you fasten the bottom of a kite to the ground, you will find that the wind will do its best to blow the kite over, and if the kite is fastened to the mast of a toy boat, the wind will try to blow the boat over.

In sailing a boat the effort of the wind apparently has but one object, and that is the upsetting of the boat. The latter, being well balanced, is constantly endeavoring to sit upright on its keel, and you, as a sailor, are aiding the boat in the struggle, at the same time subverting the purpose of the wind to suit your own ideas. It is an exciting game, in which man usually comes out ahead, but the wind gains enough victories to keep its courage up.

Every boat has peculiarities of its own, and good traits as well as bad ones, which give the craft a personal character that lends much to your interest, and even affects your sensibilities to the extent of causing you to have the same affection for a good, trustworthy craft that you have for an intelligent and kind dog or horse.

A properly balanced sail-boat, with main sheet trimmed flat and free helm, should be as sensitive as a weathercock and act like one—that is, she ought to swing around until her bow pointed right into the "eye of the wind," the direction from which the wind blows. Such a craft it is not difficult to sail, but it frequently happens that the boat that is given to you to sail is not properly balanced, and shows a constant tendency to "come up in the wind"—face the wind—when you are doing your best to keep her sails full and keep her on her course. This may be caused by too much sail aft. The boat is then said to carry a weather helm.

Weather Helm.—When a boat shows a constant tendency to come up in the wind.

Lee Helm.—When a boat shows a constant tendency to fall off the wind—that is, when the wind blows her bow to the leeward. This is a much worse trait than the former, and a boat with a lee helm is a dangerous boat. It may be possible to remedy it by adding sail aft or reducing sail forward, which should immediately be done.

In spite of the fact, already stated, that the wind's constant effort is to capsize a boat, there is little or no danger of a properly rigged boat upsetting unless the sheets are fast or hampered in some way. When a sail-boat upsets it is, of course, because the

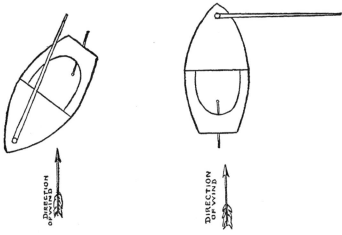

Fig. 130.—Close-hauled.   Fig. 131.—Before the wind.

Top view of boats, showing position of helm and boom.

wind blows it over. Now, the wind cannot blow a boat over unless the boat presents some surface larger than its hull for the wind to blow against, and the sail is the only object that offers enough surface to the breeze to cause an upset.

If the sheet is slackened, the sail will swing around until it flaps like a flag and only the thin edge is presented to the wind; and a boat that a flag will upset is no boat for beginners to trust themselves in. True, the boom may be very long and heavy enough to make it dangerous to let so much of it overboard, but this is seldom the case. A good sailor keeps his eyes constantly on the sails and trims them to take advantage of the slightest favorable breeze. In place of losing control of his sail by letting go the sheets he will ease the tiller so as to "spill" part of the wind that is, let the forward part, or luff, of the sail shake a bit. Or, in case of a sudden puff of wind, he may deem it necessary to "luff"—that is, let her shake—and slacken the sheets too.

Trimmed Flat.—Sheets hauled in until the boom is only a little to the leeward of the helm (Fig. 130).

Close-hauled.—Sheets trimmed flat and the boat pointing as near as possible to the eye of the wind. Then the sail cannot belly, and is called flat (Fig. 130).

To Sail Close-hauled

The skipper must watch that his sail does not flap or ripple at the throat, for that means that he is pointing too close to the wind and that some of the breeze is blowing on both sides of his sail, which even a novice can see will retard the boat.

Upon discovering a rippling motion at the luff of the sail put the helm up—that is, move the tiller a little to windward until the sail stops its flapping.

Before the Wind.—When the wind is astern; sailing with the wind; sailing directly from windward to leeward (Fig. 131).

In order to reach the desired point it is often expedient to sail before the wind, but unless the wind is light, beginners had better not try this. To sail before the wind you let your sheets out until the boom stands at *almost* right angles with the boat. Keep your eye on the sail and see that it does not flap, for if the man at the helm is careless and allows the boat to point enough away from the direction of the wind to allow the wind to get on the other side of the sail, the latter will swing around or jibe with such force as to endanger the mast, if it does not knock some one overboard.

The price of liberty is constant vigilance, and the price of a good sail is the same. I have seen a mast snapped off clean at the deck by a jibe, and once when out after ducks every one was so intent upon the game that proper attention was not paid to the sail. The wind got round and brought the boom with a swing aft, knocking the captain of our boat club overboard.

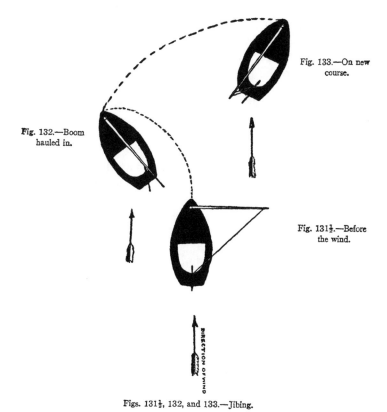

Fig. 133.—On new course.

Fig. 132.—Boom hauled in.

Fig. 131½.—Before the wind.

DIRECTION OF WIND

Figs. 131½, 132, and 133.—Jibing.

Had the boom hit him in the head and stunned him, the result might have been fatal.

Wing and Wing.—When a schooner goes before the wind with one sail out at nearly right angles on the port side and the other in the same position on the starboard side she is said to be wing and wing and presents a beautiful sight.

Tacking.—Working to the windward by a series of diagonal moves.

Legs.—The moves or diagonal courses made in tacking. It is apparent to the most unthinking observer that no vessel propelled by sail can move against the direct course of the wind—that is, nothing but electricity, naphtha, steam, or some such power can drive a boat into the eye of the wind. But what cannot be accomplished in a direct manner can be done by a series of compromises, each of which will bring us nearer to the desired point.

First we point the boat to the right or left, as the case may be, as near or as close to the wind as the boat will sail. Then we come about and sail in the other direction as close as practicable to the eye of the wind, and each time we gain something in a direct line.

When your boat changes its direction on a tack it is done by "jibing," or "coming about."

Jibing.—With the wind on the quarter, haul the main boom aft or amidship with all possible speed, by means of the main sheets (Fig. 132), and as the wind strikes the sail on the other side let it out as deliberately as possible until it reaches the position desired (Fig. 133).

Beginners should never attempt to jibe, for if there is more than a capful of wind, the sail will probably get away from them, and, as described in going before the wind, some disaster is liable to occur. Experts only jibe in light winds, and frequently lower the peak, so as to reduce sail, before attempting a jibe.

Coming About

When you wish to come about see that all the tackle, ropes, etc., are clear and in working order, and that you are making good headway; then call out: "Helm's a-lee!" or "Ready about!" and push the tiller in the direction opposite to that from which the wind blows—that is, to the lee side of the boat. This will bring the bow around until the wind strikes the sail upon the side opposite to that which it struck before the helm was a-lee (Figs. 134, 135, 136, 137).

If you are aboard a sloop or schooner, ease off the jib-sheet, but keep control of it, so that as the boat comes up to the wind you can make the jib help the bow around by holding the sheets so as

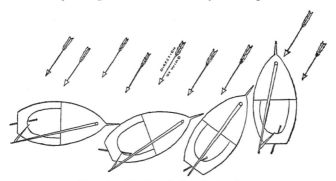

Figs. 134 135, 136, and 137.—Coming about.

to catch the wind aback. When the bow of the craft has passed the eye of the wind and the sail begins to fill give the order to make fast, or trim, the jib, and off you go upon the opposite tack, or on a new leg.

If the wind is light, or if, for any cause, the boat works slowly, you can sometimes help her by trimming in the main sheet when you let the jib-sheet fly. In the diagram of coming about no jib is shown.

Wearing is a term sometimes used in place of jibing.

In a Thunder-storm

A thunder-storm is always an uncertain thing. There may be a veritable tornado hidden in the black clouds that we see rising on the horizon, or it may simply "iron out the wind"—that is, go grumbling overhead—and leave us becalmed, to get home the best way we can; generally by what the boys call a "white-ash breeze"—that is, by using the sweeps or oars.

On Long Island Sound a thunder-storm seems to have certain fixed rules of conduct. In the first place, it comes up from the leeward, or *against the wind.* Just before the storm strikes you for an instant the wind ceases and the sails flap idly. Then look out! for in nine cases out of ten you are struck the next moment by a sudden squall from exactly the opposite direction from which the wind blew a moment before.

What to Do

Make for the nearest port with all speed, and keep a man at the downhaul ready at a moment's notice to lower sail. The moment the wind stops drop the sail and make everything snug, leaving only bare poles. When the thunder-squall strikes you, be it ever so hard, you are now in little danger; and if the wind from the new quarter is not too fresh, you can hoist sail again and make the best of your way to the nearest port, where you can "get in out of the wet."

If the wind is quite fresh keep your peak down, and with a reefed sail speed on your way. If it is a regular howler, let your boat drive before the wind under bare poles until you can find shelter or until it blows over, and the worst mishap you are likely to incur is a good soaking from the rain.

Shortening Sail.—Just as soon as the boat heels over too far for safety, or as soon as you are convinced that there is more wind than you need for comfortable sailing, it is time to take a reef— that is, to roll up the bottom of the sail to the row of little ropes, or reefing points, on the sail and make fast there. This, of course, makes a smaller sail, and that is what you wish.

While under way it will be found impossible to reef a sail except when sailing close-hauled. So the boat is brought up into the wind by pushing the helm down, as if you intended to come about. When possible it is better to lower the sail entirely before attempting to put in a reef.

To Reef Without Lowering Sail

It sometimes happens that on account of the proximity of a lee shore, and the consequent danger of drifting in that direction, or for some other equally good reason, it is inadvisable to lower sail and lose headway. Under such circumstances the main

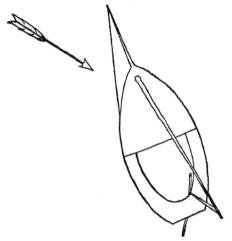

Fig. 138.—Squirming; jib on port side, boom close-hauled on starboard side.

sheet must be trimmed flat, keeping the boat as close as possible to the wind, the helm must be put up hard a-lee, and jib-sheet trimmed to windward (Fig. 138).

When this is done the wind will hit the jib, "paying her head off," or pushing her bow to leeward, and this tendency is counteracted by the helm and mainsail, bringing the bow up into the wind. This keeps the boat squirming. Lower the mainsail until the row of reef points is just on a line with the boom, keeping to the windward of the sail. Tie the first point—that is, the one on the luff rope—then the one on the leach, being careful to stretch out the foot of the sail. Then tie the remaining points, always making a square or reefing knot. Tie them to the jack-stay on the boom or around the boom.

The Reef or Square Knot

is most frequently used, as its name implies, in reefing sails. First make a plain overhand knot, as in Fig. 139. Then repeat  the operation by taking the end and passing it over and under the loop, drawing the parts tight, as shown in Fig. 140. Care should be observed in crossing the ends so that they will always lay fairly alongside the main parts. Otherwise the knot will prove a *granny* and be comparatively worthless.

Figs. 139 and 140.— Square or reef knot.

To Shake Out a Reef

untie the knots, keeping to the windward of the sail. Untie the knot at the leach first, next the one at the luff, and then the remaining points. In lowering a sail you use a rope called the **downhaul.**

Starboard Tack.—When the main boom is over the port side.

Port Tack.—When the main boom is over the starboard side.

Right of Way.—All boats sailing on the starboard tack have the right of way over all those on the port tack. In other words, if you are on the starboard tack, those on the port tack must keep out of your way. Any boat sailing close-hauled has the right of way over a boat sailing free.

Lights for Canoe

A canoe under sail at night should have an uncolored lantern hung to her mizzen-mast to notify other craft that she is out and objects to being run down. The light is put on the mizzen so that it may be behind the skipper and not dazzle him.

What you have read in the foregoing pages will not be found very difficult to remember, but there is only one way to learn to sail and that is by *sailing*. If possible, sail with some one who is a good seaman. If this sort of companion cannot be had, try it alone on smooth water and with short sail until you accustom yourself to the boat and its peculiarities. No boy ever learned to skate or swim from books, but books often have been helpful in giving useful hints to those who were really learning by practical experience.

Some Do Nots

Do not overload the boat.
Do not carry too much sail.
Do not sail in strange waters without chart or compass.
Do not forget your anchor.
Do not forget your paddles or oars.
Do not attempt to learn to sail before you know how to swim.
Do not sit on the gunwale.
Do not put the helm down too suddenly or too far.
Do not let go the helm.
Do not mistake caution for cowardice.
Do not be afraid to reef.
Do not fear the ridicule of other landlubbers.
Do not fail to keep the halyards and sheets clear.
Do not jibe in a stiff wind.
Do not fail to keep your head in times of emergency.
Do not make a display of bravery until the occasion demands it.
Do not allow mistakes or mishaps to discourage you.
Do not associate with a fool who rocks a boat.

You will soon become an expert and be able to engage in one of our most exhilarating, healthy, and manly sports and earn the proud distinction of being a good small-boat sailor.

It is Necessary to Learn to Swim

From the parents' point of view, nowhere that a boy's restless nature impels him to go is fraught with so much peril as the water, and nowhere is a boy happier than when he is on the water, unless it is when he is in it. Nowhere can be found a better school for his young mind and body than that furnished by boating. Hence it appears to be the imperative duty for parents personally to see that their children are taught to swim as soon as their little limbs have strength enough to make the proper motions.

Boating-Clothes

In aquatic sports of all kinds, if you expect to have fun, you must dress appropriately. You should have a suit of old clothes that you can change for dry ones when the sport is over. When boating, it is nonsense to pretend you can keep dry under all the varying conditions of wind and weather. If your purse is small, and you want a good rowing-suit, it can be made of last winter's woollen underclothes, and will answer for the double purpose of rowing and bathing.

How to Make a Bathing-Suit

First take an old woollen undershirt and cut the sleeves off above the elbows. Then coax your mother, aunt, or sister to sew it up in front like a sweater, and hem the edges of the sleeves where they have just been cut off.

Next take a pair of woollen drawers and have them sewed up in front, leaving an opening at the top about four inches in length; turn the top edge down all around to cover a piece of tape that should be long enough to tie in front. Have this hem or flap sewed down to cover the tape, and allow the two ends of the tape to protrude at the opening in front. The tape should not be sewed to the cloth, but should move freely, so that you can tighten or loosen it at will. Cut the drawers off at the knees and have the edges hemmed, and you will have a first-class bathing or rowing-suit.

If woollen clothes are not to be had, cotton will do, but wool is coolest and warmest, as the occasion may require.

When rowing wear old socks, woollen ones if you have them, and old shoes cut down like slippers. The latter can be kicked off at a moment's notice, and, if lost, they are of no value, and may be easily replaced.

When on shore a long pair of woollen stockings to cover your bare legs and a sweater to pull over your sleeveless shirt are handy and comfortable, but while sailing, paddling, or rowing in hot weather the rowing-suit is generally all that comfort requires. Of course, if your skin is tender, you are liable to be terribly sunburned on your arms, neck, and legs; but

Sunburn

may be avoided by gradually accustoming your limbs to the exposure. Dearly will you pay for your negligence if you go out for a day with bare arms or legs in the hot sun before you have toughened yourself, and little will you sleep that night.

I have seen young men going to business the day following a regatta with no collars on their red necks, and no shirt over their soft undershirts, the skin being too tender to bear the touch of the stiff, starched linen, and I have known others who could not sleep a wink on account of the feverish state of their bodies, caused by the hot sun and a tender skin. Most boys have had some experience from sunburn, acquired while bathing. If care is taken to cover your arms and legs after about an hour's exposure, you will find that in place of being blistered, your skin will be first pink and then a faint brownish tint, which each succeeding exposure will deepen until your limbs will assume that dark, rich mahogany color of which athletes are so proud. This makes your skin proof against future attacks of the hottest rays of the sun.

Besides the pain and discomfort of a sudden and bad sunburn on your arms, the effect is not desirable, as it is very liable to cover your arms with freckles. I have often seen men with beautifully bronzed arms and freckled shoulders, caused by going out in their shells first with short sleeves and then with shirts from which the sleeves were entirely cut away, exposing the white, tender shoulders to the fierce heat, to which they were unaccustomed.

It is a good plan to cover the exposed parts of your body with sweet-oil, vaseline, mutton-tallow, beef-tallow, or lard. This is good as a preventive while in the sun, and excellent as an application after exposure. Any sort of animal oil or grease that does not contain salt is good for your skin.

Clothes for Canoeing

In canoeing I have found it convenient to dress as I would in a shell boat, but I generally have had a sweater and a pair of long trousers stowed away, ready to be pulled on over my rowing-clothes when I landed. Once, when I neglected to put these extra clothes aboard, I was storm-bound up Long Island Sound, and, leaving my boat, I took the train home, but I did not enjoy my trip, for the bare legs and arms and knit cap attracted more attention than is pleasant for a modest man.

Do not wear laced shoes in a canoe, for experience has taught boating-men that about the most inconvenient articles of clothing to wear in the water are laced shoes. While swimming your feet are of absolutely no use if incased in this style of foot-gear, and all the work must be done with the arms. But if you have old slippers, they may be kicked off, and then you are dressed practically in a bathing-suit, and can swim with comfort and ease.

Possibly these precautions may suggest the idea that a ducking is not at all an improbable accident, and it must be confessed that the boy who thinks he can learn to handle small boats without an occasional unlooked-for swim is liable to discover his mistake before he has become master of his craft.

Stick to Your Boat

Always remember that a wet head is a very small object in the water, and liable to be passed by unnoticed, but that a capsized boat can scarcely fail to attract attention and insure a speedy rescue from an awkward position. As for the real danger of boating, it cannot be great where care is used. Not one fatality has occurred on the water, among all of my large circle of boating friends, and personally I have never witnessed a fatal accident in all the years I have spent rowing and sailing.

Life-Preservers

All canoes should have a good cork life-preserver in them when the owner ventures away from land. I never but once ventured any distance without one, and that is the only time I was ever in need of a life-preserver. The ordinary cork jacket is best. It can be used for a seat, and when spread on the bottom of your canoe, with an old coat or some article thrown over it for a cushion, it is not at all an uncomfortable seat. Most canoes have airtight compartments fore and aft—that is, at both ends—and the boat itself is then a good life-preserver. Even without the airtight compartments, unless your boat is loaded with ballast or freight, there is no danger of its sinking. A canvas canoe, as a rule, has enough woodwork about it to support your weight when the boat is full of water.

An upset canvas canoe supported me for an hour and a half during a blow on Long Island Sound, and had not a passing steamer rescued me, the canoe would evidently have buoyed me up as long as I could have held on to the hull.

CHAPTER IX

HOW TO RIG AND SAIL SMALL BOATS

How to Make a Lee-Board for a Canoe

Now that the open canvas canoe has become so popular the demand has arisen for some arrangement by which it may be used with sails. Of course it is an easy matter to rig sails on almost any sort of craft, but unless there is a keel or a centreboard the boat will make lee-way, *i. e.*, it will have no hold on the water, and when you try to tack, the boat will blow sideways, which may be fraught with serious results. The only time that the author ever got in a serious scrape with his canoe, was when he carelessly sailed out in a storm, leaving the key to his fan centreboard at the boat-house. Being unable to let down the centreboard, he was eventually driven out to sea, and when he became too fatigued to move quickly was capsized.

Now to prevent such occurrences and to do away with the inconvenience of the centreboard in an open canoe, various designs of lee-boards have been made. A lee-board is, practically speaking, a double centreboard. The paddle-like form of the blades of the boards given in Fig. 140 give them a good hold on the water when they are below the surface, and they can also be allowed to swing clear of the water when temporarily out of use. Or they may be removed and stowed away in the canoe. As you see by the diagram the two blades are connected by a spruce rod; the blades themselves may be made of some hard wood, like cherry, and bevelled at the edges like a canoe-paddle. They should be a scant foot in width and a few inches over two feet long, and cut out of three-quarter-inch material. The spruce cross-bar is about one and a half inch in diameter, the ends of which are thrust through a hole in the upper end of each lee-board. A small hole is bored in the top of each lee-board,

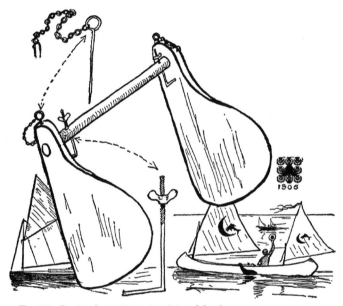

Fig. 140.—Lee-board.   Fig. 140a.—Bolt and thumb-screw.

down through the ends of the cross-board, and when a galvanized-iron pin is pushed down through this hole, it will prevent the bar from turning in its socket. A couple more galvanized-iron pins or bars fit in holes in the spruce cross-bar, as shown in the diagram (Fig. 140). At the top end of each of these metal bolts is a thumb-screw which runs down over the thread of the bolt. The bottom or lower end is bent at right angles that it may be fitted under the gunwale of the canoe, and tightened by twisting the thumb-screws. The advantage of this sort of arrangement is that the lee-boards may be slid backward or forward and so adjusted that the canoe will sail in the direction in which it is steered. The place where the lee-board is to be fastened can only be found by experiment. When it is too far toward the bow, the boat will show a desire to come up against the wind, thus making work for the steersman to keep the wind in the sails. If the lee-board is fastened too far toward the stern the canoe will show a decided determination to swing around with its stern to the wind, which is a dangerous trick for a well-trained craft to indulge in.

I have seen open canvas canoes at the outfitting stores marked as low as seventeen dollars, but they usually cost twenty-five dollars or more, and I would advise ambitious canoeists to build their own canoes, and even to make their own lee-boards, although it would be cheaper to buy the latter.

How to Rig and Sail Small Boats

To have the tiller in one's own hands and feel competent, under all ordinary circumstances, to bring a boat safely into port, gives the same zest and excitement to a sail (only in a far greater degree) that the handling of the whip and reins over a lively trotter does to a drive.

Knowing and feeling this, it was my intention to devote a couple of chapters to telling how to sail a boat; but through the kind courtesy of the editor of *The American Canoeist,* I am able to do much better by giving my readers a talk on this subject by one whose theoretical knowledge and practical experience renders him pre-eminently fit to give reliable advice and counsel. The following is what Mr. Charles Ledyard Norton, editor of the above-mentioned journal, says:

Very many persons seem to ignore the fact that a boy who knows how to manage a gun is, upon the whole, less likely to be shot than one who is a bungler through ignorance, or that a good swimmer is less likely to be drowned than a poor one. Such, however, is the truth beyond question. If a skilled sportsman is now and then shot, or an expert swimmer drowned, the fault is not apt to be his own, and if the one who is really to blame had received proper training, it is not likely that the accident would have occurred at all. The same argument holds good with regard to the management of boats, and the author is confident that he merits the thanks of mothers, whether he receives them or not, for giving their boys a few hints as to practical rigging and sailing.

In general, there are three ways of learning how to sail boats. First, from the light of nature, which is a poor way; second, from books, which is better; and third, from another fellow who knows how, which is best of all. I will try to make this article as much like the other fellow and as little bookish as possible.

Of course, what I shall say in these few paragraphs will be of small use to those who live within reach of the sea or some big lake and have always been used to boats; but there are thousands and thousands of boys and men who never saw the sea, nor even set eyes on a sail, and who have not the least idea how to make the wind take them where they want to go. I once knew some young men from the interior who went down to the sea-side and hired a boat, with the idea that they had nothing to do but hoist the sail and be blown wherever they liked. The result was that they performed a remarkable set of manœuvres within sight of the boat-house, and at last went helplessly out to sea and had to be sent after and brought back, when they were well laughed at for their performances, and had reason to consider themselves lucky for having gotten off so cheaply.

The general principles of sailing are as simple as the national game of "one ole cat." That is to say, if the wind always blew moderately and steadily, it would be as easy and as safe to sail a boat as it is to drive a steady old family horse of good and regular habits. The fact, however, is that winds and currents are variable in their moods, and as capable of unexpected freaks as the most fiery of unbroken colts; but when properly watched and humored they are tractable and fascinating playmates and servants.

Now, let us come right down to first principles. Take a bit of pine board, sharpen it at one end, set up a mast about a quarter of the length of the whole piece from the bow, fit on a square piece of stiff paper or card for a sail, and you are ready for action. Put this in the water, with the sail set squarely across (A, Fig. 141), and she will run off before the wind—which

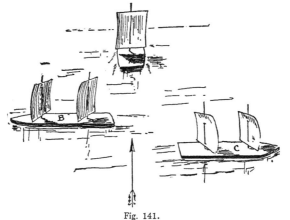

Fig. 141.
Lesson in sailing for beginners.

is supposed to be blowing as indicated by the arrow—at a good rate of speed. If she does not steer herself, put a small weight near the stern, or square end; or, if you like, arrange a thin bit of wood for a rudder.

Probably the first primeval man who was born with nautical instincts discovered this fact, and, using a bush for a sail, greatly astonished his fellow primevals by winning some prehistoric regatta. But that was all he could do. He was as helpless as a balloonist is in midair. He could go, but he could not get back, and we may be sure that ages passed away before the possibility of sailing to windward was discovered.

Now, put up or "step" another mast and sail like the first, about as far from the stern as the first is from the bow. Turn the two sails at an angle of forty-five degrees across the boat (B or C, Fig. 141) and set her adrift. She will make considerable progress across the course of the wind, although she will at the same time drift with it. If she wholly refuses to go in the right direction, place a light weight on her bow, so that she will be a little "down by the head," or move the aftermost mast and sail a little nearer to the stern.

The little rude affair thus used for experiment will not actually make any progress to windward, because she is so light that she

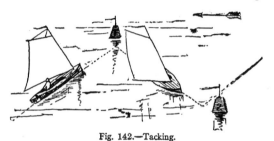

Fig. 142.—Tacking.

moves sidewise almost as easily as she does forward. With a larger, deeper boat, and with sails which can be set at any angle, the effect will be different. So long as the wind presses against the after side of the sail, the boat will move through the water in the direction of the least resistance, which is forward. A square sail having the mast in the middle was easiest to begin with for purposes of explanation; but now we will change to a "fore-and-aft" rig—that is, one with the mast at the forward edge or "luff" of the sail, as in Fig. 142. Suppose the sail to be set at the angle shown, and the wind blowing as the arrow points. The boat cannot readily move sidewise, because of the broadside resistance; she does not move backward, because the wind is pressing on the aftermost side of the sail. So she very naturally moves forward. When she nears buoy No. 1, the helmsman moves the "tiller," or handle of the rudder, toward the sail. This causes the boat to turn her head toward buoy No. 2, the sail swings across to the other side of the boat and fills on that side, which now in turn becomes the aftermost, and she moves toward buoy No. 2 nearly at right angles to her former course. Thus, through a series of zigzags, the wind is made to work against itself. This operation is called "tacking," or "working to windward," and the act of turning, as at the buoys No. 1 and No. 2, is called "going about."

It will be seen, then, that the science of sailing lies in being able to manage a boat with her head pointing at any possible angle to or from the wind. Nothing but experience can teach one all the niceties of the art, but a little aptitude and address will do to start with, keeping near shore and carrying little sail.

Simplest Rig Possible

I will suppose that the reader has the use of a broad, flat-bottomed boat without any rudder. (See Fig. 143.) She cannot be made to work like a racing yacht under canvas, but lots of fun can be had out of her.

Do not go to any considerable expense at the outset. Procure an old sheet, or an old hay cover, six or eight feet square, and experiment with that before spending your money on new material. If it is a sheet, and somewhat weakly in its texture, turn all the edges in and sew them, so that it shall not give way at the hems. At each corner sew on a few inches of strong twine, forming loops at the angles. Sew on, also, eyelets or small loops along the edge which is intended for the luff of the sail, so that it can be laced to the mast.

You are now ready for your spars, namely, a mast and a "sprit," the former a couple of feet longer than the luff of the sail, and the latter to be cut off when you find how long you want it. Let these spars be of pine, or spruce, or bamboo—as light as possible, especially the sprit. An inch and a half diameter will do for the mast, and an inch and a quarter for the sprit, tapering to an inch at the top. To "step" the mast, bore a hole through one of the thwarts (seats) near the bow and make a socket or step on the bottom of the boat, just under the aforesaid hole—or if anything a trifle farther forward—to receive the foot of the mast. This will hold the mast upright, or with a slight "rake" aft.

Lace the luff of the sail to the mast so that its lower edge will swing clear by a foot or so of the boat's sides. Make fast to the loop at D a stout line, ten or twelve feet long. This is called the "sheet," and gives control of the sail. The upper end of the sprit,

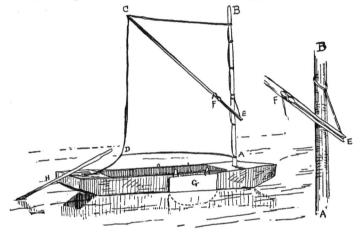

Fig. 143.—A simple rig.

C, E, is trimmed so that the loop at C will fit over it but not slip down. The lower end is simply notched to receive a short line called a "snotter," as shown in the detailed drawing at the right of the cut (Fig. 143). It will be readily understood that, when the sprit is pushed upward in the direction of C, the sail will stand spread out. The line is placed in the notch at E and pulled up until the sail sets properly, when it is made fast to a cleat or to a cross-piece at F. This device is in common use and has its advantages, but a simple loop for the foot of the sprit to rest in is more easily made and will do nearly as well. H is an oar for steering. Having thus described the simplest rig possible, we may turn our attention to more elegant and elaborate but not always preferable outfits.

Leg-of-Mutton Rig

One of the prettiest and most convenient rigs for a small boat is known as the "leg-of-mutton sharpie rig" (Fig. 144). The sail is triangular, and the sprit, instead of reaching to its upper corner, stands nearly at right angles to the mast. It is held in position at the mast by the devices already described. This rig has the advantage of keeping the whole sail flatter than any other, for the end of the sprit cannot "kick up," as the phrase goes, and so the sail holds all the wind it receives.

Fig. 144.

Fig. 145 shows a device, published for the first time in the *St. Nicholas Magazine* for September, 1880, which enables the sailor to step and unstep his mast, and hoist or lower his sail without leaving his seat—a matter of great importance when the boat is light and tottlish, as in the case of that most beautiful of small craft, the modern canoe, where the navigator sits habitually amidships. The lower mast (A, B, Fig. 145) stands about two and a half feet above the deck. It is fitted at the head with a metal ferrule and pin, and just above the deck with two half-cleats or other similar devices (A). The topmast (C, D) is fitted at F with a stout ring, and has double halyards (E) rove through or around its foot. The lower mast being in position (see lower part of Fig. 145), the canoeist desiring to make sail brings the boat's head to the wind, takes the topmast with the sail loosely furled in one hand and the halyards in the other. It is easy for him by raising this mast, without leaving his seat, to pass the halyards one on each side of the lower mast and let them fall into place close to the deck under the half-cleats at A. Then, holding the halyards taut enough to keep them in position, he will hook the topmast ring over the pin in the lower mast-heat and haul away (see top part of Fig. 145). The mast will rise into place, where it is made fast.

A collar of leather, or a knob of some kind, placed on the top-mast just below the ring, will act as a fulcrum when the halyards are hauled taut and keep the mast from working to and fro.

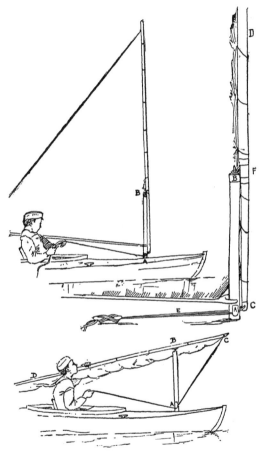

Fig. 145.—A new device.

The advantages of the rig are obvious. The mast can be raised without standing up, and in case of necessity the halyards can be let go and the mast and sail unshipped and stowed below with the greatest ease and expedition, leaving only the short lower mast standing. A leg-of-mutton sail with a common boom along the foot is shown in the cut as the most easily illustrated application of the device, but there is no reason why it may not be applied to a sail of different shape, with a sprit instead of a boom, and a square instead of a pointed head.

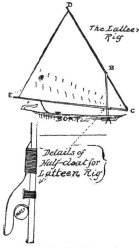

Fig. 146.—The latteen rig.

The Latteen Rig

is recommended only for boats which are "stiff"—not tottlish, that is. The fact that a considerable portion of the sail projects forward of the mast renders it awkward in case of a sudden shift of wind. Its most convenient form is shown in Fig. 146. The arrangement for shipping and unshipping the yard is precisely like that shown in Fig. 145— a short lower mast with a pin at the top and a ring fitted to the yard. It has a boom at the foot which is joined to the yard at C by means of a hook or a simple lashing, having sufficient play to allow the two spars to shut up together like a pair of dividers. The boom (C, E) has, where it meets the short lower mast, a half-cleat, or jaw, shown in detail at the bottom of the cut (Fig. 146), the circle representing a cross-section of the mast. This should be lashed to the boom, as screws or bolts would weaken it. To take in sail, the boatman brings the boat to the wind, seizes the boom and draws it toward him. This disengages it from the mast. He then shoves it forward, when the yard (C, D) falls of its own weight into his hands and can be at once lifted clear of the lower mast. To keep the sail flat, it is possible to arrange a collar on the lower mast so that the boom, when once in position, cannot slip upward and suffer the sail to bag.

The Cat-Rig

so popular on the North Atlantic coast, is indicated in Fig. 148. The spar at the head of the sail is called a "gaff," and, like the boom, it fits the mast with semicircular jaws. The sail is hoisted and lowered by means of halyards rove through a block near the mast-head. The mast is set in the bows—"Chock up in the eyes of her," as a sailor would say. A single leg-of-mutton sail will not work in this position, because the greater part of its area is too far forward of amidships. No rig is handier or safer than this in working to windward; but off the wind—running before, or nearly before it, that is—the weight of mast and sail, and the pressure of the wind at one side and far forward, make the boat very difficult and dangerous to steer. Prudent boatmen often avoid doing so by keeping the wind on the quarter and, as it were, tacking to leeward.

This suggests the question of "jibing," an operation always to be avoided if possible. Suppose the wind to be astern, and the boat running nearly before it, it becomes necessary to change your course toward the side on which the sail is drawing. The safest way is to turn at first in the opposite direction, put the helm "down" (toward the sail), bring the boat up into the wind, turn her entirely around, and stand off on the new tack. This, however, is not always possible. Hauling in the sheet until the sail fills on the other side is "jibing"; but when this happens it goes over with a rush that sometimes carries mast and sheet or upsets the boat; hence the operation should be first undertaken in a light wind. It is necessary to know how to do it, for sometimes a sail insists upon jibing very unexpectedly, and it is best to be prepared for such emergencies.

How to Make a Sail

For the sails of small boats there is no better material than unbleached twilled cotton sheeting. It is to be had two and a half of even three yards wide. In cutting out your sail, let the selvage be at the "leech," or after-most edge. This, of course, makes it necessary to cut the luff and foot "bias," and they are very likely to stretch in the making, so that the sail will assume a different shape from what was intended. To avoid this, baste the hem carefully before sewing, and "hold in" a little to prevent fulling. It is a good plan to tack the material on the floor before cutting, and mark the outline of the sail with pencil. Stout tape stitched along the bias edges will make a sure thing of it, and the material can be cut, making due allowance for the hem. Better take feminine advice on this process. The hems should be half an inch deep all around, selvage and all, and it will do no harm to reinforce them with cord if you wish to make a thoroughly good piece of work.

For running-rigging, nothing is better than laid or braided cotton cord, such as is used for awnings and sash-cords. If this is not easily procured, any stout twine will answer. It can be doubled and twisted as often as necessary. The smallest manila rope is rather stiff and unmanageable for such light sails as ours.

In fitting out a boat of any kind, iron, unless galvanized, is to be avoided as much as possible, on account of its liability to rust. Use brass or copper instead.

Hints to Beginners

Nothing has been said about reefing thus far, because small boats under the management of beginners should not be afloat in a "reefing breeze." Reefing is the operation of reducing the spread of sail when the wind becomes too fresh. If you will look at Fig. 146 you will see rows of short marks on the sail above the boom. These are "reef-points"—bits of line about a foot long passing through holes in the sail and knotted so that they will not slip. In reefing, the sail is lowered and that portion of it between the boom and the reef-points is gathered together, and the points are tied around both it and the boom. When the lower row of points is used it is a single reef. Both rows together are a double reef.

Make your first practical experiment *with a small sail and with the wind blowing toward the shore.* Row out a little way, and then sail in any direction in which you can make the boat go, straight back to shore if you can, with the sail out nearly at right angles with the boat. Then try running along shore with the sheet hauled in a little and the sail on the side nearest the shore. You will soon learn what your craft can do, and will probably find that she will make very little, if any, headway to windward. This is partly because she slides sidewise over the water. To prevent it you may use a "lee-board"—namely, a broad board hung over the side of the boat (G, Fig. 143). This must be held by stout lines, as the strain upon it is very heavy. It should be placed a little forward of the middle of the boat. It must be on the side away from the wind—the lee side—and must be shifted when you go about. Keels and centreboards are permanent contrivances for the same purpose, but a lee-board answers very well as a makeshift, and is even used habitually by some canoeists and other boatmen.

Fig. 147.—Making port.

In small boats it is sometimes desirable to sit amidships, because sitting in the stern raises the bow too high out of water; steering may be done with an oar over the lee side, or with "yoke-lines" attached to a cross-piece on the rudder-head, or even to the tiller. In this last case the lines must be rove through rings or pulleys at the sides of the boat opposite the end of the tiller. When the handle of the oar (H, Fig. 143)—or the tiller (F, Fig. 146) if a rudder is used—is pushed to the right, the boat will turn to the left, and *vice versa.* The science of steering consists in knowing when to push and how much to push—very simple, you see, in the statement, but not always so easy in practice.

The sail should be so adjusted in relation to the rest of the boat that, when the sheet is hauled close in and made fast, the boat, if left to herself, will point her head to the wind like a weather-cock and drift slowly astern. If it is found that the sail is so far forward that she will not do this, the fault may be remedied by stepping the mast further aft or by rigging a small sail near the stern. This is called a "dandy" or "steering sail," and is especially convenient in a boat whose size or arrangement necessitates sitting amidships. It may be rigged like the mainsail, and when its sheet is once made fast will ordinarily take care of itself in tacking.

Remember that, if the wind freshens or a squall strikes you, the position of safety is with the boat's head to the wind. When in doubt what to do, push the helm down (toward the sail) and haul in the slack of the sheet as the boat comes up into the wind. If she is moving astern, or will not mind her helm—and of course she will not if she is not moving—pull her head around to the wind with an oar and experiment cautiously until you find which way you can make her go.

In making a landing, always calculate to have the boat's head as near the wind as possible when she ceases to move; this whether you lower your sail or not.

Thus, if the wind is off shore, as shown at A, Fig. 147, land at F or G, with the bow toward the shore. If the wind is from the direction of B, land at E, with the bow toward B or at F; if at the latter, the boom will swing away from the wharf and permit you to lie alongside. If the wind is from D, reverse these positions. If the wind comes from the direction of C, land either at F or G, with the bow pointing off shore.

If you have no one to tell you what to do, you will have to feel your way slowly and learn by experience; but if you have nautical instincts you will soon make your boat do what you wish her to do as far as she is able. *But first learn to swim before you try to sail a boat.*

Volumes have been written on the subject treated in these few pages, and it is not yet exhausted. The hints here given are safe ones to follow, and will, it is hoped, be of service to many a young sailor in many a corner of the world.

CHAPTER X

How to Distinguish between a Ship, Bark, Brig, and Schooner—
Merits and Defects of Catboats—Advantages of the Sloop—
Rigs for Canoes—Buckeyes and Sharpies

THE two principal rigs for vessels are the fore-and-aft and the square rig.

Square rigged consists in having the principal sails extended by yards suspended at the middle (Fig. 159).

Fore-and-aft rigged is having the principal sails extended by booms and gaffs suspended by their ends (Figs. 148, 149, 150, 156, and 161).

Barks, brigs, and ships are all more or less square rigged, but schooners, sloops, and catboats are all fore-and-aft rigged. In these notes the larger forms of boats are mentioned only because of the well-known interest boys take in all nautical matters, but no detailed description of the larger craft will be given. All that is aimed at here is to give the salient points, so that the youngsters will know the name of the rig when they see it.

The Cat

There is a little snub-nosed American who, in spite of her short body and broad waist, is deservedly popular among all our amateur sailors.

The appreciation of her charms is felt and acknowledged by all her companions without envy, not because of her saucy looks, but on account of her accommodating manners.

Possessing a rare ability for quick movement, and a wonderful

power to bore her way almost into the very eye of the wind, or
with double-reefed sail to dash through the storm or gently slide
up alongside of a wharf or dock as easily as a rowboat, the American catboat, with her single mast "chock up in the eyes of her,"

Fig. 148.—The snub-
nosed American cat.

Fig. 149.—Jib and mainsail.

has made a permanent place for herself among our pleasure craft,
and is omnipresent in our crowded bays and harbors.

Knowing that there is little danger of the catboat losing its
well-earned popularity, and being somewhat familiar with many
of her peculiarities, I am free to say that this rig, notwithstanding
its numerous good points, has many serious defects as a school-

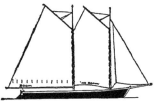

Fig. 150.—Schooner rig for open boat.
Boom on mainsail, none on foresail.

Fig. 151.—The balance lug.

ship, and the beginner had better select some other rig with which
to begin his practice sailing.

First, the great sail is very heavy and difficult to hoist and reef.
Second, in going before the wind there is constant danger of jibing, with serious results.   Third, the catboat has a very bad habit
of rolling when sailing before the wind, and each time the boat

rolls from side to side she is liable to dip the end of her heavy boom in the water and "trip herself up." When a boat trips *up* she does not necessarily go *down*, but she is likely to upset, placing the young sailors in an unenviable, if not a dangerous, position. Fourth, when the craft begins to swagger before the wind she is liable to "goose-neck"; that is, throw her boom up against the

Fig. 152.—Standing lug.

Fig. 153.—Leg-of-mutton sail.
Jib and main sail rig.

mast, which is another accident fraught with the possibilities of serious mischief.

The catboat has no bowsprit, no jib, and no topsail (Fig. 148), but that most graceful of all single-stickers,

The Sloop

possesses several jibs, a bowsprit, and topsail. Besides these, when she is in racing trim, a number of additional sails are used. All our great racers are sloops, and this rig is the most convenient for small yachts and cutters.

Racing Sloops

A racing sloop (Fig. 161) carries a mainsail, A, a fore staysail, B, a jib, C, a gaff topsail, D, a club topsail, E, a baby jib topsail, F, a No. 2 jib topsail, G, a No. 1 jib topsail, H, a balloon jib topsail, J (Fig. 157), and a spinnaker, K (Fig. 157).

Fig. 157.

Fig. 158.

Fig. 156.

Fig. 155.

Fig. 154.

Fig. 161.

Fig. 160.

Figs. 154–161.—Rigs that we meet at sea.

Fig. 159.

SLOOP

BRIG

SCHOONER

BARK

SHIP

BARKANTINE

BRIGANTINE

SLOOP

Jib and Mainsail

A small sloop's sails are a mainsail, jib, and topsail. A sloop rig without topsail is called a jib and mainsail (Fig. 149).

While every small-boat sailor should know a catboat and a sloop when he sees them, and even be able to give the proper name to their sails, neither of these rigs is very well suited for canoes, sharpies, or other boats of the mosquito fleet; but the

Schooner Rig

which is the form of boat generally used for the larger yachts, is also very much used for open boats. As you can see, by refer-

Fig. 162.—The buckeye.

Fig. 163.—The sliding gunter.

ring to Fig. 150, the schooner rig consists of a bowsprit, fore and main mast, with their appropriate sails. Lately freight schooners have appeared with four or more masts. For small boats two adjustable masts and an adjustable bowsprit, as described in the Rough and Ready, Chapter XIII, are best. The sails may be sprit sails, Figs. 164–169; balance lug, Fig. 151; standing lug, Fig. 152; leg-of-mutton, Fig. 153, or the sliding gunter, Fig. 163.

In the chapter on how to build the Rough and Ready, the sprit sail is depicted and fully described.

The Balance Lug

comes as near the square sail of a ship as any canvas used on small boats, but you can see, by referring to the diagram, Fig. 151, that the leach and the luff are not parallel and that the gaff hangs at an angle. To boom out the canvas and make it sit flat there are three sticks extended across the sail from the front to the back, luff to leach, called battens. This has caused some people to call this a batten lug. Like the lateen sail, part of the balance

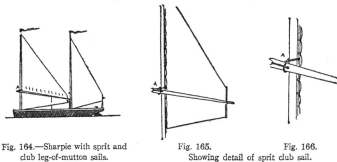

Fig. 164.—Sharpie with sprit and
club leg-of-mutton sails.

Fig. 165.

Fig. 166.
Showing detail of sprit club sail.

lug hangs before the mast and serves the purpose of a jib. This rig is said to be easily managed and to possess good sailing qualities.

The Standing Lug

is another sail approaching the square in pattern (Fig. 152), and, as any novice can see, is a good canvas with which to scud before the wind. It is very convenient for open boats built to be propelled by paddles. While the standing lug cannot point up to the eye of the wind like a schooner or cat, it is very fast on the wind or when running with the wind astern. Probably the safest form of sail used is the old reliable

Leg-of-Mutton Sail

This is used by the fishermen on their stanch little dories away up on the coast of Maine, and by the "tide-water" people in their "buckeyes" on Chesapeake Bay. The latter boat is very little known outside of the locality where it makes its home, but, like the New Haven sharpies, it is very popular in its own waters.

The Buckeye

or "bugeye," as it is sometimes vulgarly called, has a great reputation for speed and sea-going qualities. When it cannot climb a wave it goes through it. This makes a wet boat in heavy weather, but when you travel at a high rate of speed you can endure a wet jacket with no complaint, especially when you feel

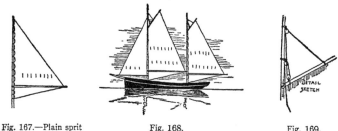

Fig. 167.—Plain sprit leg-of-mutton.

Fig. 168.
Another form of the sprit sail.

Fig. 169.

that, in spite of the fast-sailing qualities of this boat, it is considered a particularly safe craft.

The construction of a **buckeye** (Fig. 162) has been evolved from the old dugout canoe of the Indians and the first white settlers. America was originally covered with vast forests of immense trees. Remnants of these forests still exist in a few localities. It was once possible to make a canoe of almost any dimensions desired, but now in the thickly settled regions big trees are scarce.

So the Chesapeake Bay boat-builders, while still adhering to the old dugout, have overcome the disadvantage of small logs by using more than one and bolting the pieces together. Masts and sails have been added, and since the increased proportions made it impracticable to drag such a craft on the beach when in port, anchors and cables are supplied. Two holes bored, one on each side of the stem, for the cables to run through, have given the boat the appearance of having eyes, and as the eyes are large and round, the negroes called them buckeyes, and this is now the name by which all such craft are known.

At first only two masts with leg-of-mutton sails were used, but now they have a jib and two sails. With the greatest width or beam about one-third the distance from bow to stern, sharp at both ends, its long, narrow, and heavy hull is easily driven through the water and makes both a fast and stiff boat.

The buckeye travels in shallow as well as deep waters, and hence is a centreboard boat, but there is nothing unnecessary on the real buckeye—no overhanging bow or stern, for that means

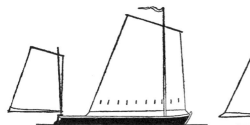

Fig. 170.—Lug rig with jigger.

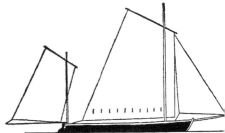

Fig. 171.—Lug rig with jigger and jib.

additional labor; no stays to the masts, for the same reason. The lack of stays to stiffen the masts leaves them with "springiness," which in case of a sudden squall helps to spill the wind and prevents what might otherwise be a "knock-down."

The foremast is longer than the mainmast and does not rake aft so much, but the mainmast has a decided rake, which the native sailors say makes the boat faster on the wind. Sometimes in the smaller boats the mainmast can be set upright when going before the wind.

Wealthy gentlemen on the Chesapeake are now building regularly equipped yachts on the buckeye plan, and some of them are quite large boats. A correspondent of the *Forest and Stream*, in speaking of the buckeye, says:

"Last summer I cruised in company with a buckeye, forty-two feet long, manned by two gentlemen of Baltimore city. She drew twenty inches without the board. In sudden and heavy flaws she was rarely luffed. She would lie over and appear to spill the wind out of her tall, sharp sails and then right again. Her crew took pleasure in tackling every sailing craft for a race; nothing under seventy feet in length ever beat her. She steered under any two of her three sails. On one occasion this craft, on her way from Cape May to Cape Charles, was driven out to sea before a heavy north-west blow. Her crew, the aforesaid gentlemen, worn out by fatigue, hove her to and went to sleep. She broke her tiller lashing during the night, and when they awoke she was pegging away

Fig. 172.—Jib.

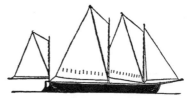

Fig. 173.—Sprit sail, schooner rig, with dandy.

on a south-east course under her jib. They put her about, and in twenty hours were inside Cape Henry, pretty well tired out. Buckeyes frequently run from Norfolk to New York with fruit. For shallow waters, I am satisfied there is no better craft afloat. Built deep, with a loaded keel, they would rival the English cutter in seaworthiness and speed."

When the hardy, bold fishermen of our Eastern States and the brave fishermen down South both use the leg-of-mutton sail, beginners cannot object to using it while practising; knowing that even if it is a safe sail, it cannot be called a "baby rig." Another safe rig, differing little from the leg-of-mutton, is the

Sliding Gunter

In this rig the sail is laced to a yard which slides up or down the mast by means of two iron hooks or travellers (Fig. 163). No sail with a narrow-pointed top is very serviceable before the wind, and the sliding gunter is no exception to the rule. But it is useful on the wind, and can be reefed easily and quickly, qualities which make it many friends.

In the smooth, shallow waters along the coast of North Carolina may be seen the long, flat-bottomed

Sharpies

Without question they are to be ranked among the fastest boats we have. These boats are rigged with a modification of the leg-of-mutton sail. The ends of the sprit in the foresail project at the

Fig. 174.—Sprit sail jib and dandy.

Fig. 175.—The lateen rig with dandy.

luff and leach. At the luff it is fastened to the mast by a line like a snotter at the leach. It is fastened to a stick sewed into the sail, called a club. The sheet is attached to the end of the sprit (Figs. 164–168).

The Sprit Leg-of-Mutton Sail

has this advantage, that the clew of the sail is much higher than the tack, thus avoiding the danger of dipping the clew in the water and tripping the boat.

The Dandy Jigger, or Mizzen Rig

is named after the small sail aft, near the rudder-head. This jigger, mizzen, or dandy may have a boom, a sprit, or be rigged as a lug. (See Figs. 170, 171, 173, 174, 175, 178, 180, and 184, which show the principal mizzen rigs in use.)

In puffy wind and lumpy water the main and mizzen rig will be found to work well. The little sail aft should be trimmed as flat as possible. It will be found of great help in beating to the windward, and will keep the nose of the boat facing the wind

Fig. 176.   Fig. 180.   Fig. 181.   Fig. 182.
Fig. 177.

Figs. 176–184.—Hybrid rigs for small boats; also two useful tackles.

Fig. 178.
Fig. 179.   Fig. 184.   Fig. 183.

when the mainsail is down.   Different rigs are popular in different localities.   For instance:

The Lateen Rig

is very popular in some parts of the Old World, yet it has only few friends here.   It may be because of my art training that I feel so kindly toward this style of sail, or it may be from association in my mind of some of the happiest days of my life with a little black canoe rigged with lateen sails.   At any rate, in spite of the undeniable fact that the lateen is unpopular, I never see a small boat rigged in this style without a feeling of pleasure.   The handy little stumps of masts end in a spike at the top and are adorned by the beautiful sails lashed to slender spars, which, by means of metal rings, are lightly, but securely, fastened to the mast by simply hooking the ring over the spike.   I freely acknowledge that when the sails are lowered and you want to use your paddle the lateen sails are in your way.   It is claimed that they are awkward to reef, and this may be true.   I never tried it.   When the wind was too strong for my sails I made port or took in either the large or the small sail, as the occasion seemed to demand.

The Ship

When you are out sailing and see a vessel with three masts, all square rigged, you are looking at a ship proper, though ship is a' word often used loosely for any sort of a boat (Fig. 159).

The bark is a vessel with square-rigged foremast and mainmast and a fore-and-aft rigged mizzen-mast (Fig. 160).

The brig is a vessel with only two masts, both of which are square rigged (Fig. 158).

The brigantine has two masts—foremast square rigged and mainmast fore-and-aft rigged (Fig. 155).

The barkentine has three masts—mainmast and mizzen-mast fore-and-aft rigged and foremast square rigged.   (See Fig. 154.)

CHAPTER XI

KNOTS, BENDS, AND HITCHES

How to Tie Knots Useful on Both Land and Water

THE art of tying knots is an almost necessary adjunct to not a few recreations. Especially is this true of summer sports, many of which are nautical or in some manner connected with the water.

Any boy who has been aboard a yacht or a sail-boat must have realized that the safety of the vessel and all aboard may be imperilled by ignorance or negligence in the tying of a knot or fastening of a rope.

With some the knack of tying a good, strong knot in a heavy rope or light cord seems to be a natural gift; it is certainly a very convenient accomplishment, and one that with practice and a little perseverance may be acquired even by those who at first make the most awkward and bungling attempts.

A bulky, cumbersome knot is not only ungainly, but is generally insecure.

As a rule, the strength of a knot is in direct proportion to its neat and handsome appearance.

To my mind it is as necessary that the archer should know how to make the proper loops at the end of his bow-string as it is that a hunter should understand how to load his gun.

Every fisherman should be able to join two lines neatly and securely, and should know the best and most expeditious method of attaching an extra hook or fly; and any boy who rigs up a hammock or swing with a "granny" or other insecure knot deserves the ugly tumble and sore bones that are more than liable to result from his ignorance.

A knot, nautically speaking, is a "bend" that is more permanent than a "hitch." A knot properly tied never slips, nor does it jam so that it cannot be readily untied. A "hitch" might be termed a temporary bend, as it is seldom relied upon for permanent service. The "hitch" is so made that it can be cast off or unfastened more quickly than a knot.

It is impossible for the brightest boy to learn to make "knots, bends, and hitches" by simply reading over a description of the methods; for, although he may understand them at the time, five minutes after reading the article the process will have escaped his memory. But if he take a piece of cord or rope and sit down with the diagrams in front of him, he will find little difficulty in managing the most complicated knots; and he will not only acquire an accomplishment from which he can derive infinite amusement for himself and a means of entertainment for others, but the knowledge gained may, in case of accident by fire or flood, be the means of saving both life and property.

The accompanying diagrams show a number of useful and important bends, splices, etc. To simplify matters, let us commence with Fig. 185, and go through the diagrams in the order in which they come:

The "English" or "common single fisherman's knot" (Fig. 185, I) is neat and strong enough for any ordinary strain. The diagram shows the knots before being tightened and drawn together.

When exceptional strength is required it can be obtained by joining the lines in the ordinary single fisherman's knot (Fig. 185, I) and pulling each of the half knots as tight as possible, then drawing them within an eighth of an inch of each other and wrapping between with fine gut that has been previously softened in water, or with light-colored silk.

An additional line or a sinker may be attached by tying a knot in the end of the extra line and inserting it between the parts of the single fisherman's knot before they are drawn together and tightened.

Fig. 185.—Some useful knots.

The "fisherman's double half knot," Fig. 185 (II and III).
After the gut has been passed around the main line and through
itself, it is passed around the line once more and through the same
loop again and drawn close.

Fig. 185 (IV, V, and IX). Here are three methods of joining the ends of two lines together; the diagrams explain them
much better than words can. Take a piece of string, try each
one, and test their relative strength.

Fig. 185 (VI). It often happens, while fishing, that a hook is
caught in a snag or by some other means lost. The diagram
shows the most expeditious manner of attaching another hook
by what is known as the "sinker hitch," described further on
(Fig. 185, D, D, D, and Fig. 186, XIV, XV, and XVI).

Fig. 185, VII is another and more secure method of attaching
a hook by knitting the line on with a succession of half-hitches.

How to Make a Horse-Hair Watch-Guard

The same hitches are used in the manufacture of horse-hair
watch-guards, much in vogue with the boys in some sections of
the country. As regularly as "kite-time," "top-time," or "ball-
time," comes "horse-hair watch-guard time."

About once a year the rage for making watch-guards used to
seize the boys of our school, and by some means or other almost
every boy would have a supply of horse-hair on hand. With the
first tap of the bell for recess, some fifty hands would dive into
the mysterious depths of about fifty pockets, and before the bell
had stopped ringing about fifty watch-guards, in a more or less in-
complete state, would be produced.

Whenever a teamster's unlucky stars caused him to stop near
the school-house, a chorus of voices greeted him with "Mister,
please let us have some hair from your horses' tails."

The request was at first seldom refused, possibly because its
nature was not at the time properly understood; but lucky was
the boy considered who succeeded in pulling a supply of hair
from the horses' tails without being interrupted by the heels of
the animals or by the teamster, who, when he saw the swarm of
boys tugging at his horses' tails, generally repented his first good-
natured assent, and with a gruff, "Get out, you young rascals!"
sent the lads scampering to the school-yard fence.

Select a lot of long hair of the color desired; make it into a switch about an eighth of an inch thick by tying one end in a simple knot. Pick out a good, long hair and tie it around the switch close to the knotted end; then take the free end of the single hair in your right hand and pass it under the switch on one side, thus forming a loop through which the end of the hair must pass after it is brought up and over from the other side of the switch. Draw the knot tight by pulling the free end of the hair as shown by Fig. 185, VII. Every time this operation is repeated a wrap and a knot is produced. The knots follow each other in a spiral around the switch, giving it a very pretty, ornamented appearance. When one hair is used up select another and commence knitting with it as you did with the first, being careful to cover and conceal the short end of the first hair, and to make the knots on the second commence where the former stop. A guard made of white horse-hair looks as if it might be composed of spun glass, and produces a very odd and pretty effect. A black one is very genteel in appearance. These ornaments are much prized by cowboys, and I have seen bridles for horses made of braided horse-hair.

Miscellaneous

Fig. 185, VIII shows a simple and expeditous manner of attaching a trolling-hook to a fish-line.

Fig. 185, F is the Blackwall hitch, used on shipboard to connect a hanging line to a hook.

Fig. 185, E is a fire-escape made of a double bow-line knot, useful as a sling for hoisting persons up or letting them down from any high place; the window of a burning building, for instance. Fig. 186, XVIII, XIX, and XX show how this knot is made. It is described on page 130.

Fig. 185, A is a "bale hitch," made of a loop of rope. To make it, take a piece of rope that has its two ends joined; lay the rope down and place the bale on it; bring the loop opposite you up, on that side of the bale, and the loop in front up, on the side of the bale next to you; thrust the latter loop under and through the first and attach the hoisting rope.   The heavier the object to be lifted, the tighter the hitch becomes.   An excellent substitute for a shawl-strap can be made of a cord by using the bale hitch, the loop at the top being a first-rate handle.

Fig. 185, B is called a cask sling, and C (Fig. 185) is called a butt sling.   The manner of making these last two and their uses may be seen by referring to the illustration.   It will be noticed that a line is attached to the bale hitch in a peculiar manner (*a*, Fig. 185).   This is called the "anchor bend."   If while aboard a sail-boat you have occasion to throw a bucket over for water, you will find the anchor bend a very convenient and safe way to attach a line to the bucket handle, but unless you are an expert you will need an anchor hitched to your body or you will follow the bucket.

Fig. 186, I and II are loops showing the elements of the simplest knots.

Fig. 186, III is a simple knot commenced.

Fig. 186, IV shows the simple knot tightened.

Fig. 186, V and VI show how the Flemish knot looks when commenced and finished.

Fig. 186, VII and VIII show a "rope knot" commenced and finished.

Fig. 186, IX is a double knot commenced.

Fig. 186, X is the same completed.

Fig. 186, XI shows a back view of the double knot.

Fig. 186, XII is the first loop of a "bow-line knot."   One end of the line is supposed to be made fast to some object.   After the turn, or loop (Fig. 186, XII), is made, hold it in position with your left hand and pass the end of the line up through the loop, or turn, you have just made, behind and over the line above, then down through the loop again, as shown in the diagram (Fig. 186, XIII); pull it tight and the knot is complete.   The "sinker hitch" is a very handy one to know, and the variety of uses it may be put to will be at once suggested by the diagrams.

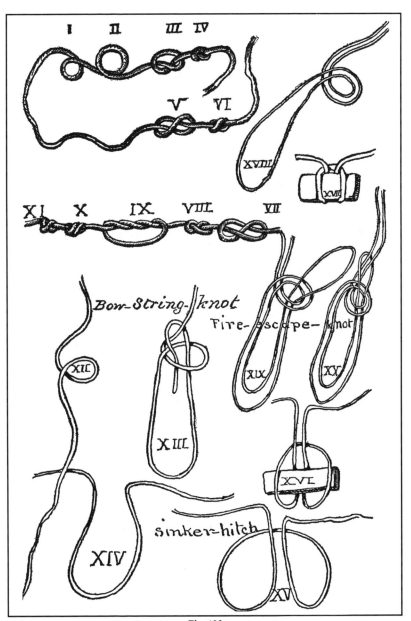

Fig. 186.

Lines that have both ends made fast may have weights attached to them by means of the sinker hitch (Fig. 185, D, D, D).

To accomplish this, first gather up some slack and make it in the form of the loop (Fig. 186, XIV); bend the loop back on itself (Fig. 186, XV) and slip the weight through the double loop thus formed (Fig. 186, XVI); draw tight by pulling the two top lines, and the sinker hitch is finished (Fig. 186, XVII).

The "fire-escape sling" previously mentioned, and illustrated by Fig. 185, E, is made with a double line.

Proceed at first as you would to make a simple bow-line knot (Fig. 186, XVIII).

After you have run the end loop up through the turn (Fig. 186, XIX), bend it downward and over the bottom loop and turn, then up again until it is in the position shown in Fig. 186, XX; pull it downward until the knot is tightened, as in Fig. 185, E, and it makes a safe sling in which to lower a person from any height. The longer loop serves for a seat, and the shorter one, coming under the arms, makes a rest for the back.

Fig. 186½, XXI is called a "boat knot," and is made with the aid of a stick. It is an excellent knot for holding weights which may want instant detachment. To detach it, lift the weight slightly and push out the stick, and instantly the knot is untied.

Fig. 186½, XXII. Commencement of a "six-fold knot."

Fig. 186½, XXIII. Six-fold knot completed by drawing the two ends with equal force. A knot drawn in this manner is said to be "nipped."

Fig. 186½, XXIV. A simple hitch or "double" used in making loop knots.

Fig. 186½, XXV. "Loop knot."

Fig. 186½, XXVI shows how the loop knot is commenced.

Fig. 186½, XXVII is the "Dutch double knot," sometimes called the "Flemish loop."

Fig. 186½, XXVIII shows a common "running knot."

Fig. 186½, XXIX. A running knot with a check knot to hold.

Fig. 186½, XXX. A running knot checked.

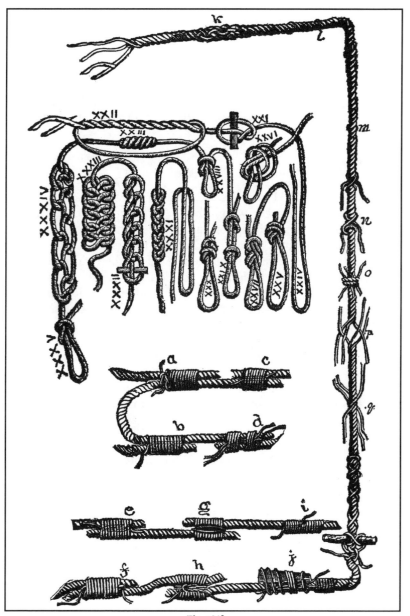

Fig. 186½.

Fig. 186½, XXXI. The right-hand part of the rope shows how to make the double loop for the "twist knot." The left-hand part of the same rope shows a finished twist knot. It is made by taking a half turn on both the right-hand and left-hand lines of the double loop and passing the end through the "bight" (loop) so made.

Whiplashes

Fig. 186½, XXXII is called the "chain knot," which is often used in braiding leather whiplashes. To make a "chain knot," fasten one end of the thong, or line; make a simple loop and pass it over the left hand; retain hold of the free end with the right hand; with the left hand seize the line above the right hand and draw a loop through the loop already formed; finish the knot by drawing it tight with the left hand. Repeat the operation until the braid is of the required length, then secure it by passing the free end through the last loop.

Fig. 186½, XXXIII shows a double chain knot.

Fig. 186½, XXXIV is a double chain knot pulled out. It shows how the free end is thrust through the last loop.

Fig. 186½, XXXV. Knotted loop for end of rope, used to prevent the end of the rope from slipping, and for various other purposes.

Splices, Timber-Hitches, etc.

Although splices may not be as useful to boys as knots and hitches, for the benefit of those among my readers who are interested in the subject, I have introduced a few bands and splices on the cables partly surrounding Fig. 186½.

Fig. 186½, *a* shows the knot and upper side of a "simple band."

Fig. 186½, *b* shows under side of the same.

Fig. 186½, *c* and *d* show a tie with cross-ends. To hold the ends of the cords, a turn is taken under the strands.

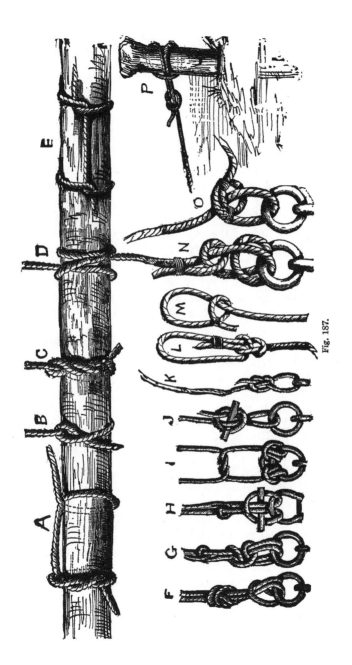

Fig. 187.

Fig. 186½, *e* and *f:*   Bend with cross-strands, one end looped over the other.

Fig. 186½, *g* shows the upper side of the "necklace tie."

Fig. 186½, *h* shows the under side of the same.   The advantage of this tie is that the greater the strain on the cords, the tighter it draws the knot.

Fig. 186½, *i* and *j* are slight modifications of *g* and *h*.

Fig. 186½, *p* shows the first position of the end of the ropes for making the splice *k*.   Untwist the strands and put the ends of two ropes together as close as possible, and place the strands of the one between the strands of the other alternately, so as to interlace, as in *k*.   This splice should only be used when there is not time to make the "long splice," as the short one is not very strong.

From *l* to *m* is a long splice, made by underlaying the strands of each of the ropes joined about half the length of the splice, and putting each strand of the one between two of the other; *q* shows the strands arranged for the long splice.

Fig. 186½, *n* is a simple mode of making a hitch on a rope.

Fig. 186½, *o* is a "shroud knot."

Fig. 186½, *r* shows a very convenient way to make a handle on a rope, and is used upon large ropes when it is necessary for several persons to take hold to pull.

Fig. 187, A.   Combination of half-hitch and timber-hitch.

Fig. 187, B.   Ordinary half-hitch.

Fig. 187, C.   Ordinary timber-hitch.

Fig. 187, D.   Another timber-hitch, called the "clove-hitch."

Fig. 187, E.   "Hammock-hitch," used for binding bales of goods or cloth.

Fig. 187, F.   "Lark-head knot," used by sailors and boatmen for mooring their crafts.

Fig. 187, P shows a lark-head fastening to a running knot.

Fig. 187, G is a double-looped lark-head.

Fig. 187, H shows a double-looped lark-head knot fastened to the ring of a boat.

Fig. 187, I is a "treble lark-head."   To make it you must first

Fig. 187¼.—Timber-hitches, etc.

tie a single lark-head, then divide the two heads and use each singly, as shown in the diagram.

Fig. 187, J shows a simple boat knot with one turn.

Fig. 187, K. "Crossed running knot." It is a strong and handy tie, not as difficult to make as it appears to be.

Fig. 187, L is the bow-line knot, described by the diagrams XII and XIII (Fig. 186). The free end of the knot is made fast by binding it to the "bight," or the loop. It makes a secure sling for a man to sit in at his work among the rigging.

Fig. 187, M, N, and O. "Slip clinches," or "sailors' knots."

Fig. 187½, Q shows a rope fastened by the chain-hitch. The knot at the left-hand end explains a simple way to prevent a rope from unravelling.

Fig. 187½, R. A timber-hitch; when tightened the line binds around the timber so that it will not slip.

Fig. 187½, S. Commencement of simple lashing knot.

Fig. 187½, T. Simple lashing knot finished.

Fig. 187½, U. "Infallible loop;" not properly a timber-hitch, but useful in a variety of ways, and well adapted for use in archery.

Fig. 187½, V. Same as R, reversed. It looks like it might give way under a heavy strain, but it will not.

Fig. 187½, W. Running knot with two ends.

Fig. 187½, X. Running knot with a check knot that can only be opened with a marline-spike.

Fig. 187½, Y. A two-ended running knot with a check to the running loops. This knot can be untied by drawing both ends of the cord.

Fig. 187½, Z. Running knot with two ends, fixed by a double Flemish knot. When you wish to encircle a timber with this tie, pass the ends on which the check knot is to be through the cords before they are drawn tight. This will require considerable practice.

Fig. 187½, a shows an ordinary twist knot.

Fig. 187½, a^1 shows the form of loop for builder's knot.

Fig. 187½, b. Double twist knot.

Fig. 187½, *c*. Builder's knot finished.

Fig. 187½, *d* represents a double builder's knot.

Fig. 187½, *e*. "Weaver's knot," same as described under the head of Becket hitch (Fig. 185, V).

Fig. 187½, *f*. Weaver's knot drawn tight.

Fig. 187½, *g* shows how to commence a reef knot. This is useful for small ropes; with ropes unequal in size the knot is likely to draw out of shape, as *m*.

Fig. 187½, *h* shows a reef knot completed.

Of all knots, avoid the "granny"; it is next to useless under a strain, and marks the tier as a "landlubber."

Fig. 187½, *i* shows a granny knot; *n* shows a granny under strain.

Fig. 187½, *j* shows the commencement of a common "rough knot."

Fig. 187½, *k*. The front view of finished knot.

Fig. 187½, *l*. The back view of finished knot. Although this knot will not untie nor slip, the rope is likely to part at one side if the strain is great. Awkward as it looks, this tie is very useful at times on account of the rapidity with which it can be made.

Fig. 187½, *o* and *p*. Knot commenced and finished, used for the same purposes as the Flemish knot.

Fig. 187½, *q* and *q¹*. An ordinary knot with ends used separately.

Fig. 187½, *s*. Sheep-shank, or dog-shank as it is sometimes called, is very useful in shortening a line. Suppose, for instance, a swing is much longer than necessary, and you wish to shorten it without climbing aloft to do so, it can be done with a sheep-shank.

Fig. 187½, *r* shows the first position of the two loops. Take two half hitches, and you have a bend of the form shown by *s*. Pull tightly from above and below the shank, and you will find that the rope is shortened securely enough for ordinary strain.

Fig. 187½, *t*. Shortening by loop and turns made where the end of the rope is free.

Fig. 187½, *u*. A shortened knot that can be used when either end is free.

Fig. 187½, *v*, *w*, and *x*.   Shortening knots.

Fig. 187½, *y* and *z*.   A "true lover's knot," and the last one that you need to practise on, for one of these knots is as much as most persons can attend to, and ought to last a lifetime.

CHAPTER XII

HOW TO BUILD A CHEAP BOAT

The Yankee Pine

FROM the saw-mills away up among the tributaries of the Ohio River come floating down to the towns along the shore great rafts of pine lumber. These rafts are always objects of interest to the boys, for the youngsters know that when moored to the shore the solidly packed planks make a splendid platform to swim from. Fine springing-boards can be made of the projecting blades of the gigantic sweeps which are used to guide the mammoth rafts, and, somewhere aboard, there is always to be found a "Yankee pine." Just when or why this style of skiff was dubbed with such a peculiar name I am unable to state; but this I know, that when a raft is to be broken up and carted away to the lumber yards there is, or always used to be, a good, light skiff to be had cheap.

However, all boys do not live on the bank of the river, and if they did there would hardly be "Yankee pines" enough to go round; so we will at once proceed to see how to build one for ourselves. Although my readers may find the "Yankee pine" a little more difficult to build than the blunt-ended, flat-bottomed scow, it really is a comparatively simple piece of work for boys familiar with the use of carpenters' tools.

For the side-pieces select two straight-grained pine boards free from knots. These boards should be about 13 or 14 feet long, a couple of inches over a foot in width, and as nearly alike as possible in texture. Besides these there should be in the neighborhood of a dozen other $\frac{3}{4}$-inch planks, an inch or two over a half foot in width. A small piece of 2-inch plank for the stern-piece is also necessary. Upon the bottom edge of the side-board measure off from each end toward the centre 4 inches, mark the points, and saw off the corners shown by the dotted line in Fig. 188. Next

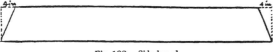

Fig. 188.—Side-board.

take a piece of board 4 feet long and a foot wide, saw off the corners as you did on the side-board, making it 4 feet on the top and 3 feet 4 inches on the bottom. This board is to be used only as a centre brace while modelling the boat.

Out of the 2-inch plank make a stern-piece of the same shape as the centre brace; let it be 1 foot wide, 14 inches long on the bottom, and 20 inches long on top. Set the side-boards on their shorter or bottom edges and place the centre brace in the middle, as shown by Fig. 189; nail the side-boards to it, using only enough nails to hold temporarily. Draw the side-boards together at the bow and against the stern-board at the stern (Fig. 189). Hold the side-pieces in position by the means of ropes. A stem should be ready to fix in the bow (Fig. 190). This had better be a few inches

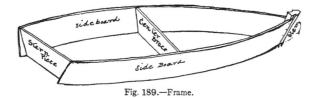

Fig. 189.—Frame.

longer than the sides are broad, as it is a simple matter to saw off the top after it is fitted. Make the stem of a triangular piece of timber, by planing off the front edge until a flat surface about $\frac{1}{2}$ inch broad is obtained; 2 inches from the front, upon each side, cut a groove just the thickness of the side-boards ($\frac{3}{4}$ inch). Trim the stem so that the side-pieces at the bow fit the grooves snugly, and nail the side-boards to the stem and to the stern-piece (Fig. 189).

Turn the boat upside down, and it will be discovered that the outlines of the bottom form an arch from stem to stern. If left in this shape the boat will sink too deep amidship. Remedy the defect by planing the bottom edge of both side pieces, reducing the convex form to

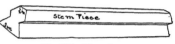

Fig. 190.—Stem-piece.

straight lines in the middle. This will allow the bow and stern to sheer, but at the same time will make the central part of the bottom flat, and, by having less to drag through the water, make it easier to row. Nail the bottom-boards on crosswise, and, as, on account of the form of the boat, no two boards will be of the same size, they must be first nailed on and the projecting ends sawed off afterward. The centre brace may now be taken out and a long bottom-board nailed to the centre of the bottom upon the inside of the boat (Fig. 191). Cut a small cross-piece

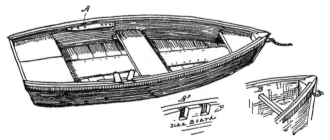

Fig. 191.—Finished skiff.

(B, Fig. 191) so that it will fit across the bow 3 inches below the top of the side-boards. Nail it in place, driving the nails from the outside of the side-board through and into the end of the stick B. Saw out a bow seat, and, allowing the broad end to rest on the cross-stick B, fit the seat in and secure it with nails (Fig. 191);

3 inches below the top of the stern-piece nail a cleat across. At the same distance below the side-board put a cross-stick similar to the one in the bow. This and the cleat on the stern-piece form rests for the stern seat. Five feet from the stern saw a notch

2 inches deep and 1½ inch long in each side-board (A, A¹, Fig. 191). Saw two more notches of the same size 3 inches from the first; these will make the rowlock when the side strips have been fastened on.

Fig. 192.—Keel board or skeg.

These strips should each be made of 1-inch plank, 2 inches wide and an inch or two longer than the side-boards. Nail the strips on the outside of the boat flush with the top of the side-boards, making a neat joint at the stern-piece ,as shown in the illustration (Fig. 191). Cut two short strips to fit upon the inside at the rowlocks and fasten them firmly on with screws (Fig. 191, A). Next cut two cleats for the oarsman's seat to rest upon. Nail them to the side-boards amidship a little nearer the bottom than the top, so that the seat, when resting upon the cleats, will be about half the distance from the top edge to the bottom of the side-boards. Let the aft end of the cleats be about 6 feet 2 inches from the stern. Make thole-pins of some hard wood to fit in the rowlocks, like those de-scribed and illustrated by Figs. 203 and 204.

The Yankee pine now only needs a skeg to complete it. This must be placed exactly in the centre, and is fastened

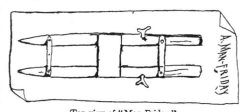

Top view of "Man Friday."

on by a couple of screws at the thin end and nails from the in-side of the boat. It is also fastened to the upright stick at the stern by screws (Fig. 192).

If the joints have been carefully made, your Yankee pine is now ready for launching. Being made of rough lumber it needs no paint or varnish, but is a sort of rough-and-ready affair, light to row; and it ought to float four people with ease. By using

planed pine or cedar lumber, and with hard-wood stem and stern, a very pretty row-boat can be made upon the same plan as a Yankee pine, or by putting in a centreboard and "stepping" a mast in the bow, the Yankee pine can be transformed into a sail-boat. But before experimenting in this line of boat-building, the beginner had better read carefully the chapter on how to rig and sail small boats.

How to Build a Better Finished Boat

The old-time raftsmen formerly built their "Yankee pines" of the rough, unplaned boards fresh from the saw-mills on the river banks, and these raw, wooden skiffs were stanch, light, and tight boats, but to-day smooth lumber is as cheap as the rough boards, so select enough planed pine lumber for a 12½-foot boat, and you may

Fig. 193.—The side-boards.

calculate the exact amount by reference to the accompanying diagrams, which are all drawn as near as may be to a regular scale.

By reference to Fig. 193 you will see that A, A represent the two

Side-Boards

These should be of sufficient dimensions to produce two side-pieces each 13 feet long, 17 inches wide, and ⅞ inch thick (A, Fig. 194). You will also need a piece for a

Spreader

54 inches long, 18 inches wide, and about 1½ inch thick, but as this is a temporary affair almost any old piece of proper dimensions will answer (B, Fig. 194), and another piece of good 1½-inch plank (C, Fig. 194) 36 inches long by 15 inches wide, for a stern-

Fig. 194.—A, the side. B, the spreader. C, the stern-piece.

piece. Besides the above there must be enough 1-inch lumber to make seats and to cover the bottom. At a point on one end, 6½ inches from the edge of the A plank, mark the point *c* (Fig. 194), then measure 37 inches back along the edge of the plank and mark the point *b* (Fig. 194). Rule a pencil line (*b*, *c*) between these two points and starting at *c* saw off the triangle *b*, *c*, *d*. Make the second side-board an exact duplicate of the one just described and prepare the spreader by sawing off the triangle with 9-inch bases at each end of B (Fig. 194). This will leave you a board (*h*, *k*, *o*, *n*) that will be 36 inches long on its lower edge and 54 inches long on its top edge.

Next saw off the corners of the stern-piece C (Fig. 194) along the lines *f*, *g*, the *g* points being each 6½ inches from the corners; and a board (*ff*, *gg*) 18 inches wide and 30 inches top measurement, with 23 inches at the bottom. Now fit the edge of the stern-piece along the line *e*, *d* (Fig. 194), or at a slant to please your fancy. In Fig. 195, upper C, the slant makes the base of the triangle about 4½ inches, which is sufficient. Be careful that both

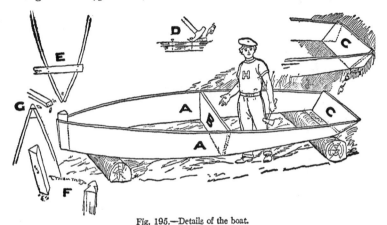

Fig. 195.—Details of the boat.

side-boards are fitted exactly alike, and to do this nail the port side with nails driven only partly in, as shown at D (Fig. 195); then nail the starboard side and, if they are both seen to be even and of the right slant, drive the nails home; if not correct, the nails may be pulled out by using a small block under the hammer (D, Fig. 195), without bending the nails or injuring the wood. Leave the stern-ends of the side-boards protruding, as in the upper C, until you have the spreader and stem in place.

We are now ready for the spreader (*h*, *k*, *o*, *n*) (B, Fig. 194) amidship, or, more accurately speaking, 6 feet 9 inches from the bow (B, Fig. 195). Nail this as shown by D (Fig. 195), so that the nails may be removed at pleasure. Bring the bow ends of the A boards together and secure them by a strip nailed temporarily across, as shown in the diagram E (Fig. 195).

The Stem-piece

may be made of two pieces, as is shown at G and F (Fig. 195),
or if you are more skilful than the ordinary non-professional, the
stem may be made of one piece, as shown by the lower diagram
at F (Fig. 195). It is desirable to have oak for the stem, but any

Fig. 196.—Put on a bottom of 1-inch boards.

hard wood will answer the purpose, and even pine may be used
when no better is to be had. Take a piece of cardboard or an old
shingle on which to draw a pattern for the end of the stem and
make the outline with a lead-pencil by placing the shingle over
the apex *c* of diagram E (Fig. 195); from the inside trace the line
of the sides thus, **V**. Trim your stem down to correspond to these
lines and let the stick be somewhat longer than the width of the
sides A, A.

When this is done to your satisfaction, fit the stem in place and
nail the side boards to the stem.

Turn the boat over and nail on a bottom of 1-inch boards as
shown by Fig. 196.

Don't

use tongue and grooved or any sort of fancy cabinet or floor joining when wet—such matched lumber warps up in waves—but
use boards with smooth, flat edges; if these are true and fitted
snugly together in workmanlike manner the first wetting will swell
them in a very short time, until not a drop of water will leak

Fig. 197.—Details of bow, stern, seats, and finished boat.

through the cracks, for the reason that there will be none. Fit
the bottom-boards on regardless of their protruding ends, as these
may be sawed off after the boards are nailed in place.

The Seats

consist of a triangular one at the bow (J), the oarsman's seat
(L), and the stern seat (K, Fig. 197). The bow seat is made of
1-inch boards nailed to two cleats shown at M (Fig. 197). N
shows the bench for the stern seat and O explains the arrangement
of the oarsman's seat a little forward amidship. As may be
seen, it rests upon the cleats x (diagram O, Fig. 197), which are
fitted between two upright cleats on each side of the boat; this
makes a seat which will not slip out of place, and the cleats serve
to strengthen the sides of the otherwise ribless boat. Make the
cleats of 1 by 2 inch lumber and let the seat be about 12 inches
wide. The stern seat may be wider, 1½ feet at K and 4 or 5 inches

more at the long sides of the two boards each side of K (Fig. 197).
Of course, it is not necessary to fit a board in against the stern-
piece, for a cleat will answer the purpose, but a good, heavy stern-
piece is often desirable and the board shown in diagram N (Fig.

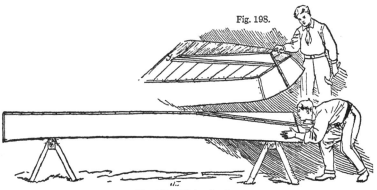

Fig. 198.

Fig. 199.—Fitting the skeg.

197) will serve to add strength to the stern as well as to furnish a
firm rest for the stern seat, but it will also add weight.

The Keel-Board

is an advisable addition to the boat, but may also be omitted without serious results (H, Fig. 197).

The keel-board should be 4½ inches wide, 1 inch thick, and
should be cut pointed, to fit snugly in the bow, and nailed in place
along the centre of the floor, before the seats are put in the boat.
A similar board along the bottom, joining the two cleats each side
of the skeg at y (Fig. 199) and extending to the bow will prevent
the danger of loosening the bottom-planks when bumping over
rifts, shallow places, or when the boat needs to be hauled on a
stony shore; this bottom-board may also be omitted to save time
and lumber, and is not shown in the diagram.

The Skeg

is a triangular board (Figs. 198 and 199), roughly speaking, of the same dimensions as the pieces sawed from the side-board *b, c, d* (Fig. 196). The stern-end will be about 7 inches wide and it will taper off to nothing at *y* (Fig. 198). The skeg is held in

Fig. 200.   Fig. 201   Fig. 202
Rowlocks.

place by cleats of 1-inch lumber, 2 inches wide, nailed to the bottom on each side of the skeg. To get the proper dimensions experiment with the pieces sawed from the A boards and cut your skeg board so that its bottom edge will be level with the bottom at *y* (Fig. 198); the diagonal line, to correspond with the slant of the stern, can be accurately drawn if the skeg is left untrimmed until it is fastened in place.

To Fasten on the Skeg

rule a line from the centre of the stern to the centre of the bow and toe-nail the skeg on along this line. This must be accurately done or you will make a boat which will have an uncomfortable tendency to move in circles. After toe-nailing the skeg to the bottom, nail the two cleats, one on each side of the skeg, and let them fit as closely as may be to the keel. Now saw off the stern-ends of the cleats and lay a rule along the stern, as the stick is placed in Fig. 198, where the boy has his finger; rule a pencil line across the protruding end of the keel and saw off the end along the diagonal line, so that the stern-cleat z (Fig. 198) may be nailed in place to finish the work.

You can buy rowlocks of galvanized iron for about a quarter of a dollar a pair; the brass ones are not expensive, but even when the store furnishes the hardware there must be a firm support of some sort to hold the rowlock.

If you use the manufactured article, to be found at any hardware store, the merchant will supply you with the screws, plates, and rowlocks, but he will not furnish you with the blocks for the holes in which the spindles of the rowlocks fit. Fig. 202 shows a rude, but serviceable, support for the lock made of short oaken posts much in vogue in Pennsylvania, but Fig. 201 is much better, and if it is made of oak and bolted to the sides of the boat it will last as long as the boat. Fig. 201 may be put upon either the outside or inside of the boat, according to the width amidship.

A Guard Rail

or fender, of 1 by 2 inch lumber, alongside of and even with the top of the side-boards, from bow to stern, gives finish and strength to the craft; but in a cheap boat, or a hastily constructed one, this may be omitted, as it is in these diagrams.

If you are building your boat out of the convenient reach of the hardware shop, you must make your own rowlocks. Fig. 200 shows the crude ones formerly used by the raftsmen for the Yankee pines, and Figs. 203 and 204 show rowlocks made with the oaken or hard-wood thole-pins fitting in holes cut for that purpose in the form of notches (U, Fig. 204) in the side of the boat, or as spaces left between the blocks, as shown by R (Fig. 203). When the side-boards A, A of the boat are notched a cleat of hard wood 5 or 6 inches wide, and extending some distance each side of the side-boards, must be used, as is shown by diagram V (Fig. 204) and Fig. 203. The diagram R (Fig. 203) explains itself; there is a centre block nailed to the side-board and two more each side, leaving spaces for the thole-pins T (Fig. 203) to fit and guarded by another piece (R) bolted through to the sides.

If bolts are out of your reach, nails and screws may act as substitutes, and Fig. 204 will then be the best form of rowlock to adopt.

To fix the place for rowlocks, seat yourself in the oarsman's seat, grasp the oars as in rowing, and mark the place which best fits the reach of your arms and oars as in rowing. It will probably be about 13 inches aft from the centre of the seat.

To Transform an Ordinary Skiff or Scow Into a Sailing-Boat

It is necessary to build the centreboard box and cut a hole through the bottom of the boat. For the average row-boat or

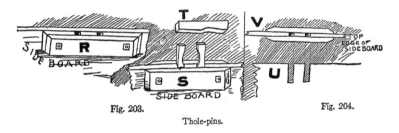

Fig. 203.   Fig. 204.

Thole-pins.

skiff, you can make the centreboard box about 48 inches long and not higher, of course, than the gunwales of the boat. Make the box of 2-inch plank, and before nailing the sides together coat the seams thoroughly with white lead so as to prevent it from leaking. The centreboard should be made of 2-inch plank, which when planed down and smoothed will be about $\frac{7}{8}$ of an inch thick, and the space in the box should be wide enough to allow it to move freely up and down, with no danger of its jamming. A hole should be cut in the bottom of the boat to correspond with the opening in the centreboard box, which, with a 48-inch box, will probably be an opening of 40 inches long and 1 inch wide. The centreboard is hinged to the box by a bolt run through at the point marked A on Fig. 205. The centreboard should move freely on the bolt, but the bolt itself should fit tightly in the sides of the box, otherwise the water will leak through. There will be no danger of the bolt's turning in its socket if the hole through the centreboard through which the bolt is thrust is made large enough. The centreboard box should be generously

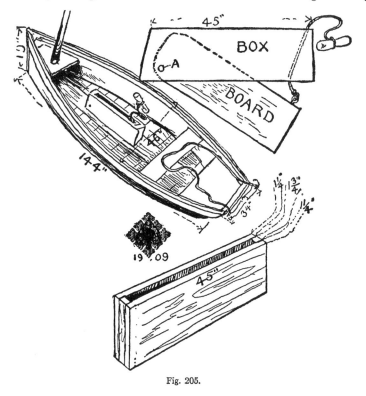

Fig. 205.

painted with white lead on the bottom edges where it fits on the floor of the boat around the centreboard hole. The bottom of the boat floor should also be coated with white lead and over this a strip of muslin spread before the box is securely nailed to the floor of the boat from the bottom or under side of the boat. When this is done the muslin covering the hole can be cut away with a sharp knife. A rope may then be fastened to the loose end of the centre-board with a cross-stick attached to the end of the rope to prevent it from slipping down the hole in the box. With this rope the centreboard may be raised or lowered to suit the pleasure of the sailor. (Fig. 205.)

CHAPTER XIII

A "ROUGH-AND-READY" BOAT

Just What One Must Do to Build It—Detailed Instructions as to How to Make the Boat and How to Rig It

GOOD straight-grained pine wood is, without doubt, the best "all-around" wood for general use. It is easily whittled with a pocket-knife; it works smoothly under a plane; can be sawed without fatiguing the amateur carpenter; it is elastic and pliable; therefore use pine lumber to build your boat.

Examine the lumber pile carefully and select four boards nearly alike. Do not allow the dealer or his men to talk you into taking lumber with blemishes. The side pieces should be of straight-grained wood, with no large knots and no "checks" (cracks) in them, and must not be "wind shaken."

Measure the wood and see that it is over twenty-two feet long by one foot four or five inches wide and one inch thick. Trim two of the side-pieces until they are exact duplicates (Fig. 206). The stem-piece (or bow-piece) should be made from a triangular piece of oak (Fig. 212), and it is wise to make it a few inches longer than will be necessary, so that there may be no danger of finding, after all your labor, that the stick is too short; much better too long, for it is a simple matter to saw it off. Make a second stem-piece (Fig. 213) of oak about one inch thick and the same length as the first, and two or three inches wide, or twice as wide as the thickness of the side-boards.

The Stern-piece

The stern-piece can be fashioned out of two-inch pine boards, and may be made as wide or narrow as you choose. A narrow

stern makes a trim-looking craft.   With your saw cut off the corner of the tail-piece, so that it will be in the form of a blunted triangle (Fig. 214), measuring three feet ten and one-half inches
across the base, three feet four inches on each side, and nine and

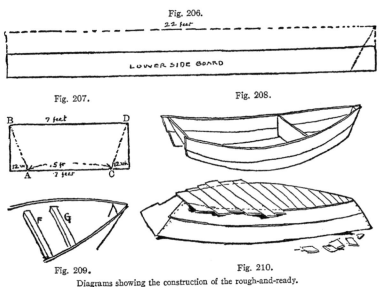

Fig. 206.

Fig. 207.

Fig. 208.

Fig. 209.

Fig. 210.

Diagrams showing the construction of the rough-and-ready.

one-half inches at the apex.   The base of the triangle will be the
top and the apex will be the bottom of the stern-board of your
boat.

Now make a brace on which to model your boat.   Let it be of
two-inch pine wood, two and one-half feet wide and seven and
one-half feet long (Fig. 207).   Measure twelve inches on one
edge of this board from each end toward the centre and mark the
points;   then rule lines from these points diagonally across the
width of the board (A, B and C, D—Fig. 207), and saw off the
corners, as shown by the dotted line in Fig. 207.

Lay the boards selected for the lower side-boards on a level floor
and measure off one and one-half foot on the bottom edge, then

in a line with the end of the board mark a point on the floor that would be the top edge of the board if the board were two and one-half feet wide; rule a line from the point on the floor to the point marked on the board and saw off the corner as marked; make the other side-piece correspond exactly with the first (Fig. 206).

Use Rope for Binding

Set the side-pieces upon their bottoms or shorter edges and place the brace between the sides. Now bind the stern ends with a rope and bring the bow-pieces together until they touch; rope them in this position, and when all is fast push the brace up until it rests at a point nine feet from the bow; fasten it here with a couple of nails driven in, but leaving their heads far enough from the wood to render it easy to draw them out. Now adjust the bow-piece, and use the greatest of care in making the sides exactly alike, otherwise you will wonder how you happened to have such an unaccountable twist in your craft. When the stem is properly adjusted fasten on the side-boards with screws. Do not try to hammer the screws in place, but bore holes first and use a screw-driver.

Take your stern-piece and measure the exact width of the stern end of the bottom-boards and mark it at the bottom of the stern-piece; or, better still, since the stern-board will set at an angle, put it temporarily in place, bind it fast with the ropes, and mark with a pencil just where the side-boards cross the ends of the stern-board. Remove the stern-board and saw out a piece one inch wide, the thickness of the bottom-board, from the place marked to the bottom of the stern-board. Because the top side-board overlaps the bottom one at the stern, there must be either a large crack left there or the stern-board notched to fit the side-boards (Fig. 214). Replace the stern-board and nail side-boards fast to it; now loosen the ropes which have held your boat in shape, and fit on the upper side-boards so that at the stern they will over-lap the lower side-boards an inch. Hold in place with your rope, then bring the bow end up against the stern-piece over the top of the lower side-board and fasten it in place with a rope.   With your carpenter's pencil mark the overlap, and with a plane made for that purpose, called a rabbet, trim down your board so that it will have a shoulder and an overlap to rest on the bottom-board, running out to nothing at the bow.   When the boards fit all right over the lower ones bind them in place and then nail them there (Fig. 208).   If you can obtain two good boards of the requisite

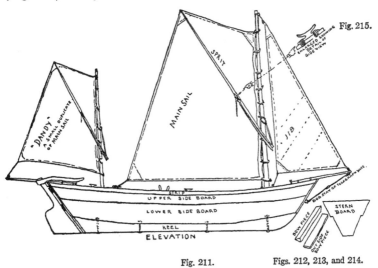

Fig. 211.
The rough-and-ready.

Figs. 212, 213, and 214.

size, you need have but one board for each side of your boat; this will obviate the necessity of using the rabbet, and be very much easier; but with single boards of the required dimensions there is great danger of splitting or cracking while bending the boards.

Planing the Bottom

Turn the boat upside down and you will see that there is a decided arch extending from stem to stern.   This would cause the boat to sink too deep amidship, and must be remedied to some extent by cutting away the middle of the arch, so that the sides in the exact centre will measure at least four inches less in width than at the bow and stern, and reducing the convex or curved form to a straight line in the middle, which will give a sheer to the bow and stern. A good plane is the best tool to use for this purpose, as with it there is no danger of cutting too deep or of splitting the side-boards. Saw off the projecting ends of the side-boards at the stern.

Make the bottom of three-quarter-inch boards, they may be bevelled like Fig. 231. Lay the boards crosswise, nail them in place, leaving the irregular ends projecting on each side. The reason for this is obvious. When you look at the bottom of the boat you will at once see that on account of the form no two boards can be the same shape, and the easiest way is to treat the boat bottom as if it were a square-sided scow. Fit the planks closely together, nail them on securely, and then neatly saw off the projecting ends (Fig. 210).

The Deck

The brace may now be removed by carefully drawing the nails, so that a bottom plank trimmed to fit the bow and the stern can be securely nailed in place (Fig. 216). Cut a notch in your brace to fit tightly over the bottom plank just laid. Plane off the top of the brace so that when in the boat the top of the brace will be four inches below the top of the side-boards. Replace the brace and securely nail it. Next cut two small cross-pieces (F, G, Fig. 209) and place them near the bow, four inches below the top of the sides of the boat. Drive the nails from the outside through the side-boards into the end of F and G, the cross-brace. Cut out a bow-piece to fit from the middle of G to the bow and nail it in place, driving the nails from the outside into the edge of the bow-piece. Fasten a small cleat along the boat from the solid board brace to F on each side and deck the space over with light lumber.

Of the same material make a trap-door to fit in between the braces F and G. This door should be big enough for a boy to reach through, for this compartment is intended as a safe place to store cooking utensils, foods, etc., as well as a water-tight compartment. At a point five feet from the stern put another cross-brace, similar to the ones in the bow, four inches below the top of the sides. At the same level nail a cleat on the stern-piece and make a stern seat by boarding over between the cross-piece and the cleat. When your boat is resting securely on the floor or level ground rig a temporary seat, then take an oar and by experiment find just where the rowlock will be most convenient and mark the spot.

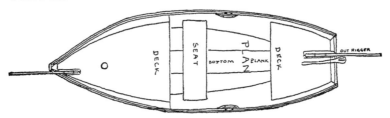

Fig. 216.—Top view of rough-and-ready, with tiller stick.

Also mark the spot best suited for the seat. On each side of the spot marked for the rowlock cut two notches in the side-boards two inches deep, one and a half inch wide, and three inches apart. Saw two more notches exactly like these upon the opposite side of your boat. These will make the rowlocks when the side-strips are nailed on (Fig. 216).

The side-strips should each be made of one-inch plank three inches wide and a few inches longer than the side-boards. Nail the strips on the outside of the boat flush with the top of the side-boards. Make your thole-pins of some hard wood, and make two sets of them while you are about it, "one set to use and one set to lose." Screw a hard-wood cleat on the inside of your boat over each pair of rowlocks, as shown in Fig. 216.

Ready for the Water

Fasten the remaining bow-piece securely over the ends of your side-boards, and the nose of your craft is finished.

Put a good, heavy keel on your boat by screwing it tightly in the stern to the hard-wood rudder-post that is fastened to the centre of the stern; bolt your keel with four iron bolts (Fig. 211) to the bottom of the boat, and the ship is ready to launch, after which she can be equipped with sails and oars.

Of course, you understand that all nail-holes and crevices should be puttied up, and if paint is used, it must be applied before wetting the boat. But if you have done your work well, there will be little need of paint or putty to make it tight after the wood has swelled in the water. Fasten your rudder on with hooks and screw-eyes, and make it as shown in the diagram (Fig. 211). Step your mainmast in the bow through a round hole in the deck and a square hole in the step, which must, of course, be screwed tightly to the bottom before the bow is decked over.

Step your jigger or dandy mast in the stern after the same manner. These masts should neither of them be very large, and are intended to be removed at pleasure by unstepping them, that is, simply pulling them out of their sockets. An outrigger will be found necessary for your dandy-sail, and since the deck aft is below the sides of the boat, a block of wood will have to be nailed to the deck to the starboard, or right-hand, side of the rudder-post. If the builder chooses, he can make the decks flush with the sides of the boat and thus avoid blocks. A couple of staples for the out-rigger to slip through are next in order. They must be fastened firmly in the block or stick of wood just nailed to the deck. A similar arrangement can be made for the bowsprit, but as it is a movable bowsprit, and the stem of the boat is in the way, put it to the port, or left-hand, side of the stem of the craft (Fig. 216).

How to Make the Sail

Secure for a sail material as strong as you can find, but it need not be heavy. Unbleached muslin is cheap and will make good sails. Turn over the edges and sew or hem them, as in the diagram. Make eyelets like button-holes in the luff of the sail—that is, the edge of the sail nearest the mast. Sew a small loop of rope in each corner of the sail. Through the eyelets lace the luff of the sail to the mast.

From spruce or pine make a sprit two inches in diameter. For a "sheet" —that is, the rope or line that you manage the sail with—tie a good stout line about a dozen feet long to the loop in the loose corner of the sail. Trim the upper end of the sprit to fit the loop in the top of the sail and make a simple notch in the other end to hold the line called the "snotter."

Now, as you can readily see by referring to Fig. 211, when the sprit is pushed into the loop at the top of the sail the sail is spread. To hold it in place make a cleat like the one in the diagram and bind it firmly with a cord to the sprit; pass the snotter, or line, fastened to the mast through the notch in the sprit up to the cleat and make fast, and the sail is set. The jigger, or dandy, is exactly like the mainsail except in size, and the sheet rope is run through a block or pulley at the end of the outrigger and then made fast to a cleat near the man at the rudder or helm. The jib is a simple affair hooked on a screw-eye in the end of the bowsprit. The jib hal-yard, or line for hoisting the jib, runs

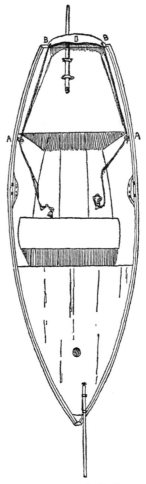

Fig. 217, with tiller.—Rudder lines.

from the top of the jib through a screw-eye in the top of the mast, down the port side of the mast to a cleat, where it is made fast. When the jib is set the jib-sheets are fastened to a loop sewed in the jib at the lower or loose end. There are two jib-sheets, one for each side of the boat, so that one may be made fast and the other loosened, according to the wind. The remaining details you must study out from the diagrams or learn by experiment.

How to Reef Her

When the wind is high reef your sails by letting go the snotter and pulling out the sprit. This will drop your peak and leave you with a simple leg-of-mutton sail. Only use the jib in light weather.

In this boat, with a little knowledge of sailing, you may cruise for weeks, lowering your sails at night and making a tent over the cock-pit for a sleeping-room. Sails with boom and gaffs may be used if desired.

CHAPTER XIV

HOW TO BUILD CHEAP AND SUBSTANTIAL HOUSE-BOATS

Plans for a House-Boat that May Be a Camp or Built as Large as a Hotel

WHEN the great West of the United States began to attract immigrants from the Eastern coast settlements, the Ohio River rolled between banks literally teeming with all sorts of wild game and wilder men: then it was that the American house-boat had its birth.

The Mississippi, Ohio, and their tributaries furnished highways for easy travel, of which the daring pioneers soon availed themselves.

Lumber was to be had for the labor of felling the trees. From the borders of the Eastern plantations to the prairies, and below the Ohio to the Mississippi, and from the Great Lakes to the Gulf of Mexico, was one vast forest of trees; trees whose trunks were unscarred by the axe, and whose tall tops reached an altitude which would hardly be believed by those of this generation, who have only seen second, third, or fourth growth timber.

When the settlement of this new part of the country began it was not long before each stream poured out, with its own flood of water,

A Unique Navy

There were keel-boats, built something like a modern canal-boat, only of much greater dimensions; there were broad-horns, looking like Noak's arks from some giant's toy-shop, and there were flat-boats and rafts, the latter with houses built on them, all recklessly drifting, or being propelled by long sweeps down the current into the great solemn, unknown wilderness.

Every island, had it a tongue, could tell of wrecks; every point or headland, of adventure.

The perils were great and the forest solemn, but the immigrants were merry, and the squeaking fiddle made the red man rise up from his hiding-place and look with wonder upon the "long knives" and their women dancing on the decks of their rude crafts, as they swept by into the unknown.

The advent of the steam-boat gradually drove the flat-boat, broad-horn, keel-boat, and all the primitive sweep-propelled craft from the rivers, but many of the old boatmen were loath to give up so pleasant a mode of existence, and they built themselves house-boats, and, still clinging to their nomadic habits, took their wives, and went to house-keeping on the bosom of the waters they loved so well.

Their descendants now form what might well be called a race of river-dwellers, and to this day their quaint little arks line the shores of the Mississippi and its tributaries.

Some of These House-Boats

are as crudely made as the Italian huts we see built along the railroads, but others are neatly painted, and the interiors are like the proverbial New England homes, where everything is spick-and-span.

Like the driftwood, these boats come down the stream with every freshet, and whenever it happens that the waters are particularly high they land at some promising spot and earn a livelihood on the adjacent water, by fishing and working aboard the other river-craft, or they land at some farming district, and as the waters recede they prop up and level their boats, on the bank, with stones or blocks of wood placed under the lower corners of their homes.

The muddy waters, as they retire, leave a long stretch of fertile land between the stranded house and the river, and this space is utilized as a farm, where ducks, chickens, goats and pigs are raised and where garden-truck grows luxuriantly.

From a boat their home has been transformed to a farm-house; but sooner or later there will be another big freshet, and when the waters reach the late farm-house, lo! it is a boat again, and goes drifting in its happy-go-lucky way down the current. If it escapes the perils of snags and the monster battering-rams, which the rapid current makes of the drifting trees in the flood, it will land again, somewhere, down-stream.

Lately, while on a sketching trip through Kentucky, I was greatly interested in these boats, and on the Ohio River I saw several making good headway against the four-mile-an-hour current. This they did by the aid of

Big Square Sails

spread on a mast planted near their bows, thus demonstrating the practicability of the use of sails for house-boats.

The house-boats to be described in this article are much better adapted for sailing than any of the craft used by the water-gypsies of the Western rivers.

For open and exposed waters, like the large lakes which dot many of our inland States, or the Long Island Sound on our coast, the following plans of the American boy's house-boat will have to be altered, but the alterations will be all in the hull. If you make the hull three feet deep it will have the effect of lowering the cabin, while the head-room inside will remain the same. Such a craft can carry a good-sized sail, and weather any gale you are liable to encounter, even on the Sound, during the summer months.

Since the passing away of the glorious old flat-boat days, idle people in England have introduced the

House-Boat as a Fashionable Fad

which has spread to this country, and the boys now have a new source of fun, as a result of this English fad.

There are still some nooks and corners left in every State in the

Union which the greedy pot-hunter and the devouring saw-mill have as yet left undisturbed, and at such places the boy boatmen may "wind their horns," as their ancestors did of old, and have almost as good a time. But first of all they must have a boat, and for convenience the American boy's house-boat will probably be

Fig. 218.—A primitive house-boat.

found to excel either a broad-horn or a flat-boat model, it being a link between the two.

The simplest possible house-boat is a Crusoe raft,* with a cabin near the stern and a sand-box for a camp-fire at the bow. A good time can be had aboard even this primitive craft. The next step in evolution is the long open scow, with a cabin formed by stretching canvas over hoops that reach from side to side of the boat (see Fig. 218).

Every boy knows how to build

A Flat-Bottomed Scow

or at least every boy should know how to make as simple a craft as the scow, but for fear some lad among my readers has neglected this part of his education, I will give a few hints which he may follow.

Building Material

Select lumber that is free from large knots and other blemishes. Keep the two best boards for the sides of your boat. With your saw cut the side boards into the form of Fig. 219; see that they are exact duplicates. Set the two pieces parallel to each other upon their straight or top edges, as the first two pieces shown in Fig. 220. Nail on an end-piece at the bow and stern, as the bumper is nailed in Figs. 221 and 222; put the bottom on as shown in Figs. 196 and 210, and you have a simple scow.

* See p. 10.

Centrepiece

In Fig. 219 you will notice that there are two sides and a centre-piece, but this centrepiece is not necessary for the ordinary open boat, shown by Fig. 218.   Here you have one of the simple forms of house-boat, and you can make it of dimensions to suit your convenience.   I will not occupy space with the details of this boat,

Fig. 219.—Unfinished.

because they may be seen by a glance at the diagrams, and my purpose is to tell you how to build the American boy's house-boat, which is a more elegant craft than the rude open scow, with a canvas-covered cabin, shown by Fig. 218.

The Sides of the House-Boat

are 16 feet long, and to make them you need some sound two-inch planks.   After selecting the lumber plane it off and make the edges true and straight.   Each side and the centrepiece should now measure exactly 16 feet in length by 14 inches in width, and about 2 inches thick.   Cut off from each end of each piece a triangle, as shown by the dotted lines at G, H, I (Fig. 220); from H to G is 1 foot, and from H to I is 7 inches.   Measure from H to I 7 inches, and mark the point.   Then measure from H to G, 12 inches, and mark the point. Then, with a carpenter's pencil, draw a line from G to I, and saw along this line. Keep the two best planks for the sides of your boat, and use the one that is left for the centrepiece. Measure 2 feet on the top or straight edge of your centrepiece, and mark the point A (Fig. 220). From A measure 8 feet 10 inches, and mark the point C (Fig. 220).

With a carpenter's square rule the lines A, B and C, D, and make them each 10 inches long, then rule the line B, D (Fig. 220). The piece A, B, C, D must now be carefully cut out; this can be done by using the saw to cut A, B and D, C. Then, about 6 inches from A, saw another line of the same length, and with a chisel cut the block out. You then have room to insert a rip-saw, at B, and can saw along the line B, D until you reach D, when the piece may be removed, leaving the space A, B, D, C for the cabin of the boat (see Figs. 221 and 222.)

At a point 9 inches from the bow of the boat make a mark on the centrepiece, and another mark 5 inches farther away, at F (Fig. 220). With the saw cut a slit at each mark, 1 inch deep, and with a chisel cut out, as shown by the dotted lines; do the same at E, leaving a space of 1½ feet between the two notches, which are made to allow the two planks shown in the plan (Fig. 221) to rest on. These planks support the deck and the hatch, at the locker in the bow. The notches at E and F are not on the side-boards, the planks being supported at the sides by uprights, Figs. 221 and 222.

All that now remains to be done with the centrepiece is to saw some three-cornered notches on bottom edge, one at bow, one at stern, and one or two amidship; this is to allow the water which may leak in to flow freely over the whole bottom, and to prevent it from gathering at one side and causing your craft to rest upon an uneven keel.

Next select a level piece of ground near by and arrange the three pieces upon some supports, as shown in Fig. 219, so that from outside to outside of side-pieces it will measure just 8 feet across the bow and stern. Of 1-inch board

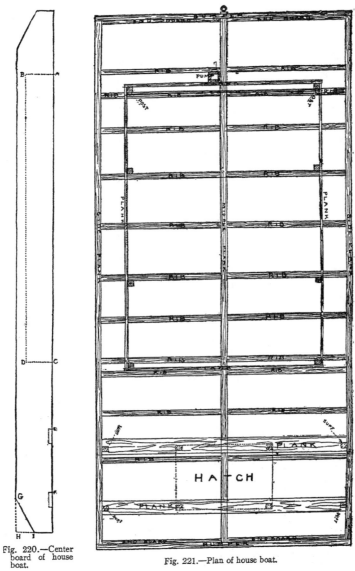

Fig. 220.—Center board of house boat.

Fig. 221.—Plan of house boat.

Make Four End-Pieces

for the bow and stern (see A, A', Fig. 219), to fit between the sides and centrepiece. Make them each a trifle wider than H, I, Fig. 220, so that after they have been fitted they can be trimmed down with a plane, and bevelled on the same slant as the bottom at G, I, Fig. 220. It being 8 feet between the outside of each centrepiece, and the sides and the centrepiece being each 2 inches thick, that gives us 8 feet 6 inches, or $7\frac{1}{2}$ feet as the combined length of A and A' (Fig. 219). In other words, each end-piece will be half of $7\frac{1}{2}$ feet long—that is, 3 feet 9 inches long. After making the four end-pieces, each 3 feet 9; by 9 inches, fit the ends in place so that there is an inch protruding above and below. See that your bow and stern are perfectly square, and nail with wire nails through the sides into A and A'; toe-nail at the centre-piece—that is, drive the nails from the broad side of A and A' slantingly, into the centrepiece, after which trim down with your plane the projecting inch on bottom, to agree with the slant of the bottom of the boat.

Now for the Bottom

This is simple work. All that is necessary is to have straight, true edges to your one-inch planks, fit them together, and nail them in place. Of course, when you come to the slant at bow and stern the bottom-boards at each end will have to have a bevelled edge, to fit snugly against the boards on the flat part of the bottom of the boat; but any boy who is accustomed to shake the gray matter in his brain can do this. Remember, scientists say that thought is the agitation of the gray matter of the brain, and if you are going to build a boat or play a good game of football you must shake up that gray stuff, or the other boys will put you down as a "stuff." No boy can expect to be successful in building a boat, of even the crudest type, unless he keeps his wits about him, so I shall take it for granted that there are no "stuffs" among my readers.

After the boards are all snugly nailed on the bottom, and fitted

together so that there are no cracks to calk up, the hull is ready to
have

The Bumpers

nailed in place, at bow and stern.   See the plan, Fig. 221, and
the elevation, Fig. 222.   The bumpers must be made of 2-inch
plank, 8 feet long by about 9 inches wide; wide enough to cover

Fig. 222.—Cross-section of boat.

A and A′ of Fig. 219, and to leave room for a bevel at the bottom
edge to meet the slant of the bow and stern, and still have room
at the top to cover the edge of the deck to the hull (see Fig. 222).

The Hull May Now Be Painted

with two coats of good paint, and after it is dry may be turned
over and allowed to rest on a number of round sticks, called rollers.

If you will examine Fig. 221 you will see there

Twenty-Odd Ribs

These are what are called two-by-fours—that is, 2 inches thick
by 4 inches wide.   They support the floor of the cabin and forward locker, at the same time adding strength to the hull.

The ribs are each the same length as the end-board.   A and A′
of Fig. 219, are nailed in place in the same manner.   Each

bottom-rib must have a notch 2 inches deep cut in the bottom edge to allow the free passage of water, so as to enable you to pump dry. Commencing at the stern, the distance between the inside of the bumper and the first rib is 1 foot 6 inches. This is a deck-rib, as may be seen by reference to Figs. 221 and 222. After measuring 1½ foot from the bumper, on inside of side-board, mark the point with a carpenter's pencil. Measure the same distance on the centrepiece, and mark the point as before; then carefully fit your rib in flush or even with the top of the side-piece, and fasten it in place by nails driven through the side-board into the end of the rib, and toe-nailed to centrepiece. Do the same with its mate on the other side of centrepiece.

The Cabin of this House-Boat

is to fit in the space, A, B, D, C of the centrepiece, Fig. 220. There is to be a one-inch plank at each end (see Fig. 222), next to which the side-supports at each end of cabin fit. The supports are two-by-twos; so, allowing 1 inch for the plank and 2 inches for the upright support, the next pair of ribs will be just 3 inches from A B, Fig. 220, of the centrepiece (see Figs. 221 and 222). The twin ribs at the forward end of the cabin will be the same distance from D C, Fig. 220, as shown in the plan and elevation, Figs. 221 and 222. This leaves five pairs of ribs to be distributed between the front and back end of the cabin. From the outside of each end-support to the inside of the nearest middle-support is 2 feet 6 inches. Allowing 2 inches for the supports, this will place the adjoining ribs 2 feet 8 inches from the outside of the end-supports. The other ribs are placed midway between, as may be seen by the elevation, Fig. 222.

There is another pair of

Deck-Ribs

at the forward end of the cabin, which are placed flush with the line D, C, Fig. 220 (see Figs. 221 and 222). The two pairs of ribs in the bow are spaced, as shown in the diagram. This description may appear as if it was a complicated affair; but you will find it a simple thing to work out if you will remember to allow space for your pump in the stern, space for the end-planks at after and forward end of cabin, and space for your uprights. The planks at after and forward end of cabin are to box in the cabin floor.

The Boat May Now Be Launched

by sliding it over the rollers, which will not be found a difficult operation.

The Plans Show Three Lockers

—two in the bow under the hatch and one under the rear bunk— but if it is deemed necessary the space between-decks, at each side of the cabin, may be utilized as lockers. In this space you can store enough truck to last for months. A couple of doors in the plank at the front of the cabin opening, under the deck, will be found very convenient to reach the forward locker in wet weather.

The Keel

is a triangular piece of 2-inch board, made to fit exactly in the middle of the stern, and had best be nailed in place before the boat is launched (see Fig. 222). The keel must have its bottom edge flush with the bottom of the boat, and a strip of hard-wood nailed on the stern-end of the keel and bumper, as shown in the diagram. A couple of strong screw-eyes will support the rudder.

After the boat is launched the

Side-Supports for the Cabin May Be Erected

These are "two-by-twos" and eight in number, and each 5 feet 9 inches long. Nail them securely at their lower ends to the adjoining ribs. See that they are plumb, and fasten them temporarily with diagonal pieces, to hold the top ends in place, while you nail down the lower deck or flooring.

Now fit and nail the two 1-inch planks in place, at the bow and stern-end of the cabin, each of which has its top one inch above the sides, even with the proposed deck (see dotted lines in Fig. 222).

Use Ordinary Flooring

or if that is not obtainable use ¾-inch pine boards, and run them lengthwise from the bow to the front end of the cabin and along the sides of the cabin. Then floor the cabin lengthwise from bow to stern. This gives you a dry cabin floor, for there are 4 inches of space underneath for bilge-water, which unless your boat is badly made and very leaky, is plenty of room for what little water may leak in from above or below. The two side-boards of the cabin floor must, of course, have square places neatly cut out to fit the uprights of the cabin. This may be done by slipping the floor-board up against the uprights and carefully marking the places with a pencil where they will come through the board, and then at each mark sawing two inches in the floor plank, and cutting out the blocks with a chisel.

The Hatch

Now take a "four-by-four" and saw off eight short supports for the two 1-inch planks which support the hatch, Figs. 221 and 222. Toe-nail the middle four-by-four to the floor in such a position that the two cross-planks (which are made to fit in the notches E and F, Fig. 220) will rest on the supports. Nail the four other supports to the side-boards of your boat, and on top of these nail the cross-planks, as shown in the diagrams.

The boat is now ready for its

Upper Deck

of 1-inch pine boards. These are to be nailed on lengthwise, bow and stern and at sides of cabin, leaving, of course, the cabin open, as shown by the position of the boys in Fig. 222, and an opening, 3 feet by 2, for the hatch (Fig. 221). The two floors will act as benches for the uprights of the cabin, and hold them stiff and plumb.

To further stiffen the frame, make two diagonals for the stern-end, as shown in Fig. 223, and nail them in place.

The Rafters

or roof-rods, should extend a foot each way beyond the cabin, hence cut them two feet longer than the cabin, and after testing

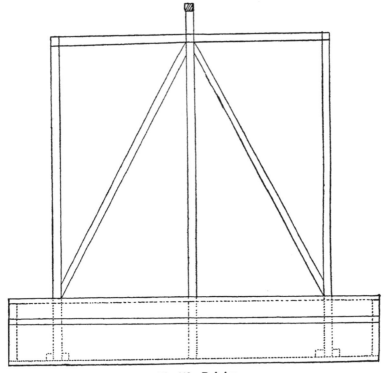

Fig. 223.—End view.

your uprights, to see that they are exactly plumb, nail the two side roof-rods in place (see dotted lines in Fig. 222). The cross-pieces at the ends, as they support no great weight, may be fitted between the two side-rods, and nailed there.

The roof is to be made of ½-inch boards bent into a curve, and the ridge-pole, or centre roof-rod, must needs have some support. This is obtained by two short pieces of 2 by 4, each 6 inches long, which are toe-nailed to the centre of each cross-rod, and the ridge-pole nailed to their tops. At 3 feet from the upper deck the side frame-pieces are toe-nailed to the uprights. As may be seen, there are three two-by-fours on each side (Fig. 222).

The space between the side frame-pieces, the two middle uprights, and side roof-rods, is where the windows are to be placed.

Use ½-inch (tongue and groove preferred) pine boards for sidings, and

Box In Your Cabin

neatly, allowing space for windows on each side, as indicated. Leave the front open. Of the same kind of boards make your roof; the boards being light you can bend them down upon each side and nail them to the side roof-rods, forming a pretty curve, as may be seen in the illustration of the American boy's house-boat.

This Roof

to be finished neatly and made entirely water-proof, should be covered with tent-cloth or light canvas, smoothly stretched over and tacked upon the under side of the projecting edges. Three good coats of paint will make it water-proof and pleasant to look upon.

The description, so far, has been for a neatly finished craft, but I have seen very serviceable and comfortable house-boats built of rough lumber, in which case the curved roof, when they had one, had narrow strips nailed over the boards where they joined each other or was covered with tar-paper.

To Contrive a Movable Front

to your cabin, make two doors to fit and close the front opening, but in place of hanging the doors on hinges, set them in place. Each door should have a good strong strap nailed securely on the inside, for a handle, and a batten or cross-piece at top and bottom of inside surface. A $1\frac{1}{2}$ by 4, run parallel to the front top cross-frame and nailed there, just a sufficient distance from it to allow the top of the door to be inserted between, will hold the top

Fig. 224.—End view.

of the door securely. A two-by-four, with bolt-holes near either end to correspond with bolt-holes in the floor, will hold the bottom when the door is pushed in place, the movable bottom-piece shoved against it and the bolts thrust in (see Fig. 225, view from inside of cabin. Fig. 226, side view). It will be far less work to break in the side of the cabin than to burst in such doors, if they are well made. These doors possess this advantage: they can be removed and used as table-tops, leaving the whole front open to the summer breeze, or one may be removed, and still allow plenty of ventilation. A moulding on deck around the cabin is not necessary, but it will add finish and prevent the rain-water from leaking in.

To lock up the boat you must set the doors from the inside,

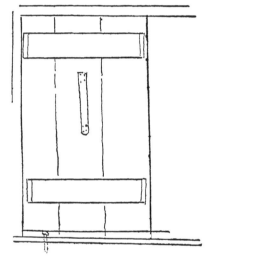

Fig. 225.—Inside view of door.

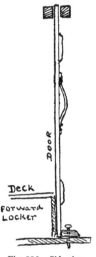

Fig 226.—Side view of door.

and if you wish to leave the craft locked you must crawl out of the window and fasten the latter with a lock.

Fig. 227 shows the construction of

The Rudder

and also an arrangement by which it may be worked from the front of the boat, which, when the boat is towed, will be found most convenient.

The hatch should be made of 1-inch boards, to fit snugly flush with the deck, as in the illustration, or made of 2-inch plank, and a moulding fitted around the opening, as shown in Fig. 222.

A Pair of Rowlocks

made of two round oak sticks with an iron rod in their upper ends, may be placed in holes in the deck near the bow, and the boat can be propelled by two oarsmen using long "sweeps," which have holes at the proper places to fit over the iron rods projecting from the oaken rowlocks.   These rowlocks may be removed when not

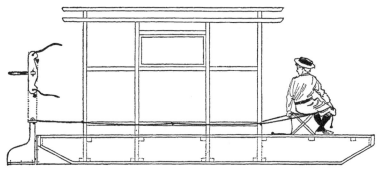

Fig 227.—Side elevation.

in use, and the holes closed by wooden plugs, while the sweeps can be hung at the side of the cabin, under its eaves, or lashed fast to the roof.

Two or More Ash Poles

for pushing or poling the boat over shallow water or other difficult places for navigation are handy, and should not be left out of the equipment.   The window-sashes may be hung on hinges and supplied with hooks and screw-eyes to fasten them open by hooking them to the eaves when it is desired to let in the fresh air.   All window openings should be protected by wire netting to keep out insects.

Two bunks can be fitted at the rear end of the cabin, one above the other, the bottom bunk being the lid to a locker (see Fig. 222).

The Locker

is simply a box, the top of which is just below the deck-line and extending the full width of the cabin.   It has hinges at the back, and may be opened for the storage of luggage.

Over the lid blankets are folded, making a divan during the day and a bed at night.

The top bunk is made like the frame of a cheap cot, but in place of being upholstered it has a strong piece of canvas stretched across it.   This bunk is also hinged to the back of the cabin, so that when not in use it can be swung up against the roof and fastened there as the top berth in a sleeping-car is fastened.   Four 4 by 4 posts can be bolted to the side-support at each corner of the bottom bunk; they will amply support the top bunk, as the legs do a table-top when the frame is allowed to rest upon their upper ends.   This makes accommodation for two boys, and there is still room for upper and lower side bunks, the cabin being but six feet wide.   If you put bunks on both sides you will be rather crowded, it is true, but by allowing a 1-foot passage in the middle, you can have two side bunks and plenty of head room. This will accommodate four boys, and that is a full crew for a boat of this size.

On board a yacht I have often seen four full-grown men crowded into a smaller space in the cabin, while the sailormen in the fo'-castle had not near that amount of room.

A More Simple Set of Plans

Here the cabin is built on top of the upper deck, and there are no bottom-ribs, the uprights being held in place by blocks nailed to the bottom of the boat, and by the deck of the boat.   This is secure enough for well-protected waters, small lakes, and small streams.   Upon the inland streams of New York State I have seen two-story house-boats, the cabin, or house, being only a framework covered with canvas.   One such craft I saw in central New York, drifting downstream over a shallow riff, and as it bumped along over the stones it presented a strange sight. The night was intensely dark, and the boat brightly lighted. The lights shone through the canvas covering, and this big, luminous house went bobbing over the shallow water, while shouts of laughter and the "plinky-plunk" of a banjo told in an unmistakable manner of the jolly time the crew were having.

Canvas-Cabined House-Boat

If you take an ordinary open scow and erect a frame of uprights and cross-pieces, and cover it with canvas, you will have just such a boat as the one seen in central New York. This boat may be propelled by oars, the rowers sitting under cover, and the canvas being lifted at the sides to allow the sweeps to work; but of course it will not be as snug as the well-made American boy's house-boat, neither can it stand the same amount of rough usage, wind, and rain as the latter boat.

In the frontispiece the reader will notice a stove-pipe at the stern; there is room for a small stove back of the cabin, and in fair weather it is much better to cook outside than inside the cabin. When you tie up to the shore for any length of time, a rude shelter of boughs and bark will make a good kitchen on the land, in which the stove may be placed, and you will enjoy all the fun of a camp, with the advantage of a snug house to sleep in.

For the benefit of boys who doubt their ability to build a boat of this description, it may be well to state that other lads have used these directions and plans with successful results, and their boats now gracefully float on many waters, a source of satisfaction and pride to their owners.

Information for Old Boys

On all the Western rivers small flat-boats or scows are to be had at prices which vary in accordance with the mercantile instincts of the purchaser, and with the desire of the seller to dispose of his craft. Such boats are propelled by "sweeps," a name used to designate the long poles with boards on their outer edges that serve

as blades and form the oars.   These boats are often supplied with
a deck-house, extending almost from end to end, and if such a
house is lacking one may be built with little expense.   The cabin
may be divided into rooms and the sleeping apartments supplied
with cheaply made bunks.   It is not the material of the bunk
which makes it comfortable—it is the mattress in the bunk upon
which your comfort will depend.   The kitchen and dining-room
may be all in one.   An awning spread over the roof will make a
delightful place in which to lounge and catch the river breezes.

The Cost of House-Boats

The cost of a ready-made flat-bottomed house-boat is anywhere
from thirty dollars to one or more thousands.   In Florida such a
boat, 40 by 20 feet, built for the quiet waters of the St. John's
River or its tributaries, or the placid lagoons, will cost eight hundred dollars.   This boat is well painted outside and rubbed down
to a fine oil finish inside; it has one deck, and the hull is used for
toilet apartments and state-rooms; the hull is well calked and all
is in good trim.   Such expense is, however, altogether unnecessary —there need be no paint or polish.   All you need is a well-
calked hull and a water-tight roof of boards or canvas overhead;
cots or bunks to sleep in; chairs, stools, boxes or benches to sit
on; hammocks to loll in, and a good supply of provisions in
the larder.

House-boats for the open waters are necessarily more expensive.
As a rule they need round bottoms that stand well out of the water,
and are built like the hull of a ship.   These boats cost as much to
build as a small yacht.   From twelve to fifteen hundred dollars
will build a good house-boat, with comfortable sleeping-berths,
toilet-rooms and store-rooms below; a kitchen, dining-room, and
living-rooms on the cabin deck, with wide, breezy passageways
separating them.

If a bargain can be found in an old schooner with a good hull,
for two or three hundred dollars, a first-class house-boat can be
made by the expenditure of as much more for a cabin.   The roofs

of all house-boats should extend a foot or more beyond the sides of the cabin.

For People of Limited Means

For people with little money to spend, these expensive boats are as much out of reach as a yacht, but they may often be rented for prices within the means of people in moderate circumstances. At New York I have known a good schooner-yacht, 84 feet over all, to be chartered for two weeks, with crew of skipper and two men, the larder plentifully supplied with provisions and luxuries for six people and the crew, making nine in all, at a cost of thirty-six dollars apiece for each of the six passengers. An equally good house-boat should not cost over twelve dollars a week per passenger for a party of ten. In inland waters, if a boat could be rented, the cost should not exceed seven or eight dollars a week per passenger.

A canal-boat is a most excellent house-boat for a pleasure party, either on inland streams or along our coast.

Street-Car Cabins

Since the introduction of cable and trolley-cars the street-car companies have been selling their old horse-cars, in some instances at figures below the cost of the window-glass in them; so cheap, in fact, that poor people buy them to use as woodsheds and chicken-coops.

One of these cars will make an ideal cabin for a house-boat, and can be adapted for that purpose with little or no alterations. All it needs is a good flat-boat to rest in, and you have a palatial house-boat.

CHAPTER XV

A CHEAP AND SPEEDY MOTOR-BOAT

How To Build the Jackson Glider—A Very Simple Form of Motor-Boat, Which Will Hold Its Own in Speed With Even Expensive Boats of Double Horse-Power

THIS boat is intended to slide over the top of the water and not through it, consequently it is built in the form of a flat-bottom scow. Order your wood dressed on both sides, otherwise it will come with one side rough. For the side-boards we need two pine, or cedar boards, to measure, when trimmed, 14 feet (Fig. 228), and to be 16 or 18 inches wide.

The Stern-Board

when trimmed, will be 2½ feet long by 1 foot, 8½ inches wide. It may even be a little wider, because the protruding part can be planed down after the boat is built (Fig. 229).

To make the bow measure from the point E (Fig. 228) 1 foot 8½ inches and mark the point C. Measure along the same line 13½ inches and mark the point D. Next measure from B down along the edge of the boat one inch and mark the point F. Again measure down from B, 5¾ inches and mark the point G. With a carpenter's pencil draw the lines F D and G C and saw these pieces off along the dotted line (Fig. 232). The bow can then be rounded at the points A and B with a sharp knife or jackplane.

To get the proper slant on the stern, measure from H 4½ inches to L and saw off the triangle LHK. Make the other side board an exact duplicate of the first one, as in Fig. 228. Next set these two boards on edge, like sledge runners (Fig. 230), and let them

184

be 2 feet, 6 inches apart (the boat will be safer if made six inches wider, and its speed will be almost as great), which can be tested by fitting the stern-boards between them before nailing the temporary boards on, which are to hold them in place (Fig. 230). Do

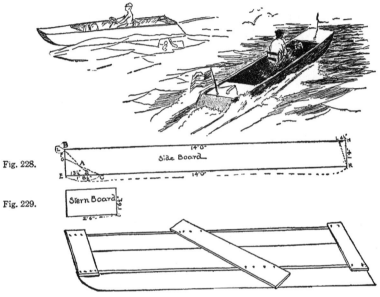

Fig. 228.

Fig. 229.

Fig. 230.—Parts of motor-boat.

not drive the nails home, but leave the heads protruding on all temporary braces, so that they may be easily removed when necessary.

Now turn the boat bottom side up and nail the bottom on, as already described in previous chapters (Fig. 232). The bottom-boards are to be so planed upon their edges that they leave V-shaped grooves on the inside of the boat to be calked with candle-wick and putty (Fig. 231). Next make a shaft-log by cutting a board in a trianguiar piece, as shown in Fig. 233, and nailing two other pieces of board on it, and leaving a space for the shaft-rod, over which is nailed a duplicate of the bottom-board, as shown in Fig. 234. Make the shaft-log of three thicknesses of 1-inch plank. To make it more secure there should be a board nailed on the inside bottom of the boat, as shown in Fig. 235 by the dotted lines.

This board is put there to strengthen the bottom and allow us to cut a slot through for the admission of a shaft (Fig. 236) which

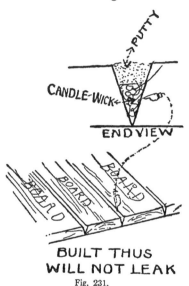

BUILT THUS
WILL NOT LEAK

Fig. 231.

is drawn on a scale shown below it. With the engine comes a stuffing box, through which the shaft passes and which prevents the water from coming up through the shaft-hole. The stuffing boxes, which are furnished to fit upon the inside of the boat, are expensive, but one to fit upon the stern of the shaft-log costs but little, and will answer all purposes.

Of course, when attaching the shaft-log to the bottom, it must be in the exact centre of the boat. Find the centre of the boat at the bow and stern, mark the points and snap a chalk-line between them. Now place the shaft-log in position on this line and while holding that there firmly, mark around it with a carpenter's pencil. Next lay the shaft-log flat on its side with its edge along this line and with your pencil mark on the bottom of the boat the exact place where the shaft-hole must be cut to correspond with the one in the shaft-log. As may be seen by Fig. 236, the shaft runs through at an acute angle; hence the hole must be bored on a slant, or better still a slot cut through the floor long enough to allow for the slant.

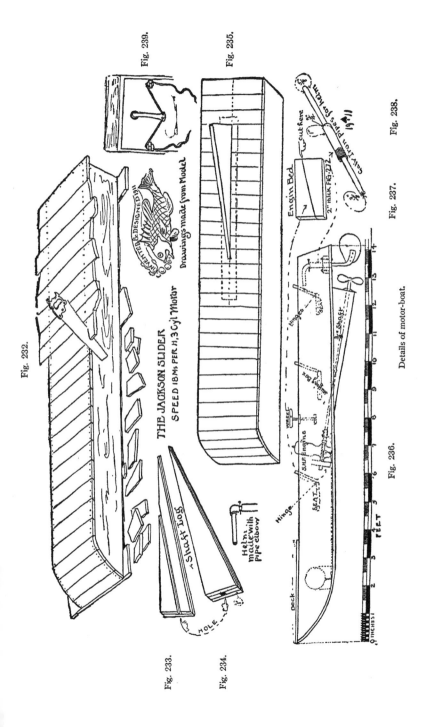

Fig. 239.

Fig. 235.

Fig. 232.

THE JACKSON SLIDER
SPEED 18 M.s PER H. 3 Cyl Motor

INVENTED & DESIGNED 1911

Drawings made from Model

Engin Bed

2" Thick FiG. 222.

Galv. Iron pipes for horn

cut here

Fig. 238.

Fig. 237.

Shaft Log

Helm.
made with
Pipe elbow

HOLE

Fig. 233.

Fig. 234.

DECK

HINGE

SEAT ½ H.

5 H.P. Engine

WHEEL

eng engine

Rog Exhaust

SEAT

HINGES

SHAFT

INCHES

FEET

Fig. 236.

Details of motor-boat.

The leak, which would naturally occur here is prevented by the stuffing box which is fastened on to the stern-end of the shaft-log where the latter protrudes for the propeller. To set the engine in the boat it is necessary to have an engine-bed. This is made of two pieces of board cut diagonally, upon which the engine rests.

Fig. 237 shows a piece of 2-inch board and a method of sawing it to make the duplicate pieces to form the engine-bed. The dimension of these pieces must be obtained by measuring the width of the engine rest, which is to be installed. The angle, of course, must correspond to the angle of the shaft.

Make your own rudder of any shape that suits your fancy, square or paddle-shaped, of a piece of galvanized iron or of wood, as shown in the diagram; or you can simply fasten the rudder-stem to the transom (stern-board), as is often done on row-boats and sail-boats. If you desire to make your rudder like the one shown here, use two pieces of galvanized pipes for your rudder-posts, one of which fits loosely inside of the other. Make the rudder-posts of what is known as $\frac{3}{8}$-inch (which means literally a $\frac{3}{8}$-inch opening) and for its jacket use a $\frac{3}{4}$-inch pipe, or any two kinds of pipe, which will allow one to turn loosely inside the other. The smaller pipe can be bent easily by hand to suit your convenience, after it has been thrust through the larger pipe.

First bend the lower end of the small pipe to fit your proposed rudder, then remove the larger pipe and flatten the lower end of the small one by beating it with the hammer. To bore the screw-holes in the flattened end you will use a small tool for drilling metal. One of these drills, which will fit any carpenter's brace, can be procured for the cost of a few cents.

Drill holes through the flattened end of your pipe for the reception of your screws, which are to secure it to the rudder. It is now necessary to fasten a block of 2-inch plank securely to the bottom of the boat upon the inside where the rudder-post is to be set. This block might best be secured on with four bolts. A hole is then bored through the block and the bottom of the boat a trifle smaller than the largest piece of pipe; the latter is supposed to have screw threads upon its lower end (Fig. 238) so that it may be screwed into the wood, but before doing so coat the threads with white lead and also the inside of the hole in the block with the same substance.

When the larger pipe is now screwed into the block until its lower end is flushed with the outside bottom of the boat, the white lead will not only make the process easier, but will tend to keep out the moisture and water from the joint.

From the outside thrust the upper end of the small pipe through the hole in the bottom until it protrudes the proper distance above the larger pipe, and with the point of a nail scratch a mark on the surface of the small pipe where it issues from the big one. At this point drill a hole through the small pipe to admit a nail which is to act as a peg to keep the helm from sliding down and jamming in its bearings.

If you choose, a small seat or deck may be inserted in the stern, through which the helm extends and which will help to steady it. The top of the helm, or protruding ends of the small pipe may now be bent over toward the bow, as shown in the diagram, and by holding some hard substance under it, the end may be flattened with a hammer and two holes drilled through the flattened end for the rudder-line, as in Fig. 239. These lines work the rudder and extend on each side of the boat through some clothes-lines pulleys, as shown in Fig. 239.

If you slice off the ring from a common rubber hose and slip it over the inside pipe before you fasten it in place, it will prevent the water from spurting up through the rudder pipe when the boat is speeding.

Any boat will leak if not carefully built and the simplest kind of a craft carefully put together is as water-tight as the most finished and expensive boat.

For a gasoline tank any good galvanized iron vessel will answer if it holds five gallons or more of gasoline. It can be placed in the bow on a rest made for it. Of course the bottom of the tank must be on a level or higher than the carburetor of the engine; the tank is connected by a small copper, or block-tin pipe, which you procure with the engine.

This boat, if built according to plans, should cost ten dollars or less, not counting the cost of the engine. The cost of the latter will vary according to the style of one you use, and whether you get it first or second hand.

A ten-horse power engine drove a boat of this kind at the rate of eighteen miles an hour.

For beginners, this is as far as it is safe to go in boat-building, but thus far any one with a rudimentary knowledge of the use of tools can go, and, if one has followed the book through from chapter to chapter he should be a good boat-builder at

The End